Defeating the Giant

Defeating the Giant

A Guide to Recognizing and Healing from Narcissistic Abuse

Rosanne Nunnery

ROWMAN & LITTLEFIELD
Lanham • Boulder • New York • London

Published by Rowman & Littlefield
An imprint of The Rowman & Littlefield Publishing Group, Inc.
4501 Forbes Boulevard, Suite 200, Lanham, Maryland 20706
www.rowman.com

86-90 Paul Street, London EC2A 4NE

British Library Cataloguing in Publication Information available

Library of Congress Cataloging-in-Publication Data

ISBN 978-1-5381-9553-6 (cloth)
ISBN 978-1-5381-9554-3 (paperback)
ISBN 978-1-5381-9555-0 (ebook)

~

Contents

CHAPTER 1

~

Reclaiming Yourself Following NPD Exposure

A *Personal Reflection*

For as long as I can remember, I have been different—or, rather, I felt and thought I was different when I was sitting at a restaurant, standing in a crowd, walking through school, sitting in a church pew, standing in front of a class and teaching, or sitting at the dinner table, amid other people. I am not saying I did not experience life or that I was standing back and judging others. No. I was always judging *myself*, asking, "What is wrong with me?" I pondered whether I was really supposed to be in my family or a part of my generation and even if I was meant to exist in any specific place and time. My thoughts were always analytical and existential. After doing my own personal work in counseling through meditation and mindfulness, as well as engaging in spiritual practice, reading, education, and journaling, I remain analytical and self-reflective. We all want to know who we are, and we want a sense of belonging. I can say, even now, I do not feel settled in a group and always can see beyond myself. I am not saying that I have been depersonalized either, but there seems to be a disconnect between who I am as a wife, mother, educator, and counselor and what I know in my very being. Who I am is all mixed up in all of these roles, and yet I do not identify with any one of them.

As I was pondering how to share my story regarding exposure to narcissistic abuse, I honestly was dumbfounded about where to even begin. I've written down glimpses into my life, using short stories that accumulated into what has become a memoir. We understand that memoirs are communicated from the perspective of the writer, and there are many folks within those stories who will readily reject the author's version of events. As a counselor and educator, I know that we all have our own truth. As someone who is dialectical, I can easily view issues from multiple perspectives. When engaging with a rational person, it's easy to have a dialectical dialogue, but it is not easy or even possible with someone with narcissistic traits. Within a relationship with a narcissist, the only perspective that counts is that of the narcissist.

As a child and now an adult, I often justify the actions of others, and I know it is due to my own narcissistic abuse. I've excused others' behaviors away, trying to see from the perspective of my exposure. I would say my mother's behavior was due to her upbringing, that she'd had it worse than me, and would give multiple chances and forgiveness (even when I was never asked for forgiveness), and I stayed within the relationship until I finally had to disconnect. So what is wrong with me? Nothing—and yet everything! It depends upon who is asked: the abused or the abuser.

I was born the only child of my father and the fourth child of my mother. Of course, I had very little recollection of my young life, as I was swept off at 6 weeks old to England and then to a life of travel, for I was the child of a military father. I have good and bad memories. For years I'd realized that I would mostly tell only good memories because my brain had focused on those, and then later, I realized this was due to my blocking all the traumatic memories. So I think it is only fair to explore the positive memories amid the negative ones as a means of understanding the mistakes I have made and who I am today. I know that because I had so many mixed memories and experiences, I excused all the events that were harmful, even declaring as a teenager that I never get angry, that I have the best family, and that the behavior toward me just could not be helped. Well, some things can be helped, and other things cannot.

My positive memories are linked back to images of playing dolls with my sister, riding bikes with my brothers, singing and dancing to the show *Solid Gold*, and recording tapes off the radio to listen to later. There were Barbie dolls, Cabbage Patch Kids, and scary movies; there was playing outside until the streetlights came on and living in places that some folks could only dream to ever visit in their life. I had a lot of freedom as a young child— sometimes too much freedom—with many self-reflective moments in my life. I never remember not having food on the table or a place to live, although there were luxuries we could not have. But being a United States Air Force kid opened up a world of military bases, travel, food, friends, and exploration. For a long time, I focused on how I had reaped the benefits of my parents' marriage, for my siblings had experienced many difficult situations prior to my birth. My awareness of and reflection on events really did not start until I could step out of my pretend (delusional!) version of events that I'd created in my head and could then see the reality of events from an adult perspective. Sometimes, these realities would come in glimpses or flashes, whereas others come very clearly, with details that are too difficult to forget. I was struck by a statement my husband has said to me throughout our marriage: "You always tell me the stories about when you were living in Germany." I would often say that it was because it was my favorite place to live, and it was, but I realize it was also because those held some of my happiest memories. As I looked closer, I realized even those were tainted by memories of pain and heartache. For many years, this led to me wondering if there was something wrong with me or something wrong with my family. The reality is likely both.

Memories are powerful, and some of them we want to capture and get back and dream about, while others we want to forget. One early memory included a sense that I was very close to my mother, even more so than my father. I felt closest to my middle brother and, at times, my sister, as they would play with me. As I aged, I realized my sister was stuck with me a lot of the time due both to our age and that Mom needed a babysitter. My father was always gone, but when he was home, I truly enjoyed getting to watch him build things, wiring electronics, and working with photography, but mostly, he was at temporary duty for the military. This left us children with Mom while he was gone, which created this reality that I felt closest to my mom. She was the primary caregiver. However, amid those times, scattered events occurred that shaped me and impacted my identity, especially my sense of self and belonging within the family and even within the world.

My father was the disciplinarian and was trained to use the belt, which is quite common in Southern religious culture. "Spare the rod and spoil the child" was an often-used ideology in our family; it was a fear-based method of discipline that would happen from time to time, though in the beginning, I remember my brothers getting more spankings than I did, and it always made me cringe. I always hated seeing them—or anyone—in pain. I am still like that to this day. I would say that I had a healthy fear of my father and his belt, but what I really should have feared was my mother, with her emotional abuse and manipulation.

The manipulation began very young, with subtle statements like, "Say you will never leave me. Your brothers left me; say you will never leave me." I would oblige and say, "I will never leave you, Mom." And I'd continue to play. These demands first began being sprinkled throughout my childhood when my oldest brother left home for college. Then as time progressed, I was inundated by the flood of verbal and sometimes physical abuse my mother unloaded on my father when he'd come home from temporary duty, or even just a long shift at the military base. I saw images of her belittling him, of her unreasonable demands, when she expected things of him that he could not meet and he was thus doomed to fail. As a child, I could merely go outside and play, ignoring it, or I drown it out with preoccupying activities. I know you are reading this and wondering about actual stories. Well, there are far too many to share, but following is a glimpse into a few as I break them down across varied ages.

As I noted earlier, Germany was such a beautiful place to me, filled with beautiful memories of snow, friends, playing, and just being a kid. I would walk to school with my sister while my brothers took a bus to their middle and high schools. We would learn the German language, as well as spend days enjoying the weather, the toys, and laying on the ground, looking at the sky and watching the clouds pass over. I was about 8 years old, and in the present, I am actually quite shocked at how much unsupervised time I'd had, not even coming home until the streetlights would come on, which was around 10:00 p.m. We would come home only for supper, then go back out again.

I recall how important it was in our family to eat every bit of our food—and the dinnertime fights. We had a large family, so any food on our plate was considered like a delicacy, and it could not be wasted. The problem was in how my mom controlled us: the amount on our plate, the type of food we had, and how our behavior unfolded at the table. Until the time when I'd leave home at 17, all my memories at the table consisted of arguments, belittling comments, and my mom always letting my father know how all of his behaviors were a problem: how he ate, how he chewed, the way he sat, what he wore, and the list goes on. It was all a problem to her. Even at that young age of 8, I remember wanting to eat and then leave the table. My mom could give my father a look, and he would jump. When I say jump, I mean that he's immediately jump up and do what she'd told him to do. Over time, I'd also learn what her looks meant and how I'd need to jump. He could look at her and know when he needed to shut up, get up, stop chewing, stop eating, yell at one of us kids, or clean the kitchen. Over time, I would begin to feel pity for my father, but at the time, this seemed normal to me. In fact, I never thought it was an issue. It was just normal that Mom was in charge. It was normal for my sister and I to occasionally have some chores of washing dishes and clothes and that my brothers would take out the trash. I would often prefer not to eat at the table, because, as time progressed in our apartment in Germany, there was more tension, problems, and anger. Food became an issue that would progress throughout my life.

Once or twice a week, we would load up in our van and head to a nearby city in Germany where there was a large military base, and we would purchase groceries. I have many memories of the drive to the base, with my mom screaming at my father as he drove along the mountain roads. I would sit in the back, listening to my mom yell at my dad, and I would interject, begging them to stop fighting, but it never worked. I was told to shut up and sit back down in the van. My dad would be screamed at for not driving right, the grocery list, the money, his work, and so on—all before we ever got to the base commissary. There were many moments of Mom telling Dad to stop the van, get out, and walk back home. I would beg her to go back and get him, which she'd refuse. Her nasty comments then turned to me—that is, until I shut up. There were times Mom would drive back and pick him up, but other times, she acted as though there were not three feet of snow outside. I would cry and beg, but I quickly learned it would not work and often found that the only way to have peace was to side with my mom.

The worst memories were after my dad would go into the base grocery store and bring the food back to the van. My mom made my dad do it all. She may have shopped some, but I know he got the groceries to the van, stacked them in the back, and handed my mom the items she wanted. Sometimes, my mom would demand that she drive; other times, she'd demand him to. I remember my dad being so excited about something special he would buy for my mother and making sure to tell her how he'd purchased all the items on the list. He would be glowing. Unfortunately, I knew her berating was coming. She would pause and always find something he'd missed. She would say, "Did you get this or that?" He would say, "No, it was not on the list." Immediately, the screaming would begin, and it would become so intense that he would say he'd go back in and purchase it. Of course, she would tell him it was too late and that we just needed to drive home. He was set up to fail no matter what he did. As he'd drive, my mom would pout and say nasty comments under her breath while us kids would play; sometimes we'd try to distract her because we knew there would be no good outcome if she remained focused. I would feel the anxiety rising in my body and know my mom was going to blow her top. Well, it would always happen as we were driving back home, an hour and a half around a snowy mountain. She would ask Dad why he'd not gone back and gotten the item. My dad would say, "You told me not to." Well, this was not the right answer. She would immediately tell him to stop the van, get out, and walk home. This pattern was so common, and yet it was emotionally overwhelming. He would have gone back and bought the item, and we could have driven home in peace, but Mom could never let there be peace. I always would beg to go back into the store, beg them to let me get the item. It was a twisted, manipulative, and complicated mind game. I would constantly be asking my mom to please go back and get Dad, to please stop fighting, and I would even beg her, saying that I'd go buy whatever item was missing. I learned quickly that I needed to side with Mom if I wanted to survive and not bear the brunt of her yelling and blame. This became so common that I hated grocery day or any event when we had to travel.

In the 1980s it was a big deal to have a new VCR. I remember Dad being excited to go pick one up for our family. At that time, folks would share movies/videos, and having a VCR was a big deal. My dad had worked all day and then taken the van to get the newest VCR. My dad was brilliant with electronics, fixing items, and building, and I liked to watch him work on them. I remember it being a very snowy day, Dad arriving with the VCR, and all of us watching him set it up. We were so excited, but then Dad said we could not use it that day, because a cord was missing. Well, immediately my mother began belittling him, and she told him to go back. I knew that if he went back, it would be an hour-and-a-half drive, and it was senseless to go right back since we could go tomorrow. I can still see the image of Mom yelling at Dad, saying he was stupid because he didn't have what he needed to set up the VCR. Dad was standing up, and Mom was yelling at him, while I sat on the couch, watching my dad. There'd been a window behind him, with snow falling in the background. She said, "You are not taking the van. You have to take the military bus." The bus only left and returned at specific times of the day, so he would have to leave immediately to catch the last bus. I begged Mom not to make him go, but my words were ignored. Even at the age of 8, I knew this was not right and that my dad should stand up for himself. I did not know why he would not stand up for himself. If my mom wanted something, she demanded it, and my father obliged. There were so many different times that these types of events happened.

Once we'd left Germany (not at the desire of my father but at the demand of my mother), I was older and had become more aware of my mom's behavior: her control and the trickle-down effect it had on us kids were evident. My oldest brother was of age and left Germany, moving back to the United States. And after we'd returned to the United States, it was not long before my second brother left home. Then my dad, sister, and I were the only remaining targets of her wrath. This began with her again begging me—and even my sister—to never leave her. Both our brothers had left home after graduation to head to college, which is normal. At that time, I'd not realized the depth of the many experiences and stories that had impacted my brothers. Once we'd gotten back to the United States, my dad was no longer in the military, and it was very hard for my family to financially function, which led to our return to our home state and to my dad's family's inherited land. It was not where I wanted to be, but I did have cousins and friends to hang out with during the summer and after school. It was during this time, between the ages of 11 and 13, that two major events happened to me that changed my life forever.

The first event related to my father and his motorcycle. He was a bit of a rebel, which I really liked about him. He may not have stood up to my mom, but he had his outlet: riding a motorcycle, and he loved it. It was common for my dad to allow me to ride with him on his motorcycle. He would pick me up after school, take me to the doctor, or just take a ride on his own to enjoy the sunshine and breeze.

One specific day, my dad rode from one city to the next at the request of my mother, who'd asked him to help her mother do some repairs. And I wanted to go with him; I loved how riding was a great outlet and something we could do together. He was headed to my grandmother's house to do some repairs, which was quite common. It was rare for him to have downtime, but he also enjoyed doing electronic work as a hobby. He was a natural, and I wish I could have learned more from him, even though I did not get a lot of time to engage, nor did he offer to teach me. After two trips back and forth, from city to city, I decided to stay home and hang out with my cousins, playing handball. It was about an hour later that I saw my uncle's truck come up the driveway: it had my father's motorcycle in its back. I knew it was dad's, and when I saw it, I immediately fainted. My aunt and uncle told me that my dad had been in a motorcycle wreck. Immediately after that, my mom drove in, picked me up, and took my sister and I to the hospital. I do not remember much of the ride to the hospital, but I do remember getting there. My dad was in the emergency room, and when we all arrived, I knew I wanted to see him. My mom looked at me as we waited to go in, then told me, "This is your fault. You caused him to be tired and distracted and to wreck." My eyes teared up as she walked away to see my dad, and I could hear them arguing in his hospital room. I was mortified that my mom would argue with my dad while he was so injured. My mom walked out and told me to go in and see him while quickly reiterating, "This is your fault." I walked in at my mom's insistence, and he was covered in blood with bandages. He immediately said, "Get her out of here." My mom refused, and I teared up. So did my dad, and in looking at him, I was quickly reminded that the accident was my fault. It was so traumatic to see my father like that, and I held on to that guilt until I was almost forty years old. Instead of love, empathy, and support for my dad (or me), my mother had brought nothing but blame and hate, along with a reminder to my dad that he was no longer allowed to have a motorcycle. This was the moment my dad lost his voice, the right to his opinion in our house, and most of his engagement with me, his daughter.

That same year, after the severe wreck, my dad was still in the hospital, and I was staying with my sister and her boyfriend at our house. The first night was awkward, as my sister did not want me at the house, since she and her boyfriend were there together. I called the hospital and talked to my mom, checking in on my dad. Mom said I had to stay at my grandmother's house, down the road. This was my paternal grandmother, which seemed fine to me, as I had spent all day at her house, playing handball with family and friends outside, and had been doing a lot with the aunts and grandmother who lived there. Little did I know that I was walking into a traumatic event.

I rode my bicycle down to my grandmother's house; my grandmother, aunts, uncle, and I ate supper; and then we all were watching television, while my sister stayed at our house with her boyfriend. I was enjoying a show when, slowly, my uncle began to sexually assault me. It started with him tickling me, and this led to my aunts holding me down. My grandmother watched from the other room but took no action to stop the abuse; rather, she contributed to it. I have commonly said that after this event, I've never slept soundly again. I laid on the floor in a sleeping bag, staring at the ceiling, completely awake. The next morning, I avoided my uncle and tried to stay away until my dad and mom arrived home. Unfortunately, my uncle followed me to my house later that day and trapped me in my front yard, where he assaulted me again. Now as I look back, I remember how I used redirection to get him to stop and also how I disassociated, focusing my vision on the odometer and the interior roof of the truck as it all unfolded. I was able to effectively get away and get into the house, but I was having a hysterical reaction, which triggered my mom and sister asking what was wrong with me. I did not want to say anything, because I wanted to protect my dad from all of this. My mom verbally pushed me until I told, but then I was immediately told it was no big deal, that my uncle was just mentally slow and did not know what he was doing. My father was tearful and told my mom he would kill my uncle. She quickly turned and looked at my dad as he laid in the recliner with stitches and an arm sling, with elevated limbs, and said, "You will not. No way." She demanded he do nothing about what happened and even that he allow my uncle to come to our house that night—and many nights after that. She quickly revealed that her childhood was far worse than mine, saying, "This is nothing, I experienced worse. You won't tell anyone." After this incident, my mom controlled all interactions between my dad and me. Our attachment and bond were severed due to my mom's complete control of our father-daughter relationship.

At this point it might be important to pause. I know *I* need a pause, as whenever I write or think about this, I typically end up dreaming about some version of these events. You may be thinking, "This is a negligent parent!" And she is, but you might also be wondering how this is narcissism. Well, at the time, I did not think about this as narcissism. It was very normal for me. Narcissists will do almost anything to pull any negative attention off themselves and to minimize any attention that would be on others. As I indicated, she minimized my abuse while highlighting her own stories. There was no empathy demonstrated, and her power and control over my father were evident. Even though I was in severe emotional pain, there was no consideration of my needs, never considered protecting me. Later in life, when I confronted my mother, she immediately said that I was wrong, that the event never happened, and that if it had, she would have called the police. This behavior is clearly gaslighting, as she was trying to make me question my memory of the series of events.

As I aged while living at home, I learned that to give an opinion, to hold a perspective different than my mom's, or to spend time visiting or talking with anyone in my family was against my mom's rules. After my dad's motorcycle wreck and my experience of sexual abuse, my father abruptly decided that he was being called to higher cause, to be a minister. This was a whirlwind shift from the military life to one of ministry, which led us to a move from one city to another so my father could serve at a church. It felt like being in the military, except that we'd stayed within the same state. Amid this transition, it seemed as if our family were living a lie. There was the behavior at home and the behavior as soon as we stepped out of the car and through the church doors. There were patterns in our home that I did not understand and, at times, was too embarrassed to let anyone know about. There were the constant arguments between my parents, as well as my mom's paranoia about folks in the church, her blaming them for her perceived wrong treatment, her gossiping about others, and her forcing her perceptions upon my sister, Dad, and I.

When we first got a church assignment and had moved into a parsonage, folks came and brought us food and greetings, and they even helped us set up the house. It was very warm and welcoming. As the weeks progressed, my mom grew frustrated and resentful of the church members, and if someone came to the house, she would tell us not to answer, to pretend we were not home, and to hide. This bizarre cycle then progressed to her closing all the blinds, keeping the lights off, and as soon as they'd left, her criticizing them. If my sister and I were to answer the door, we'd experience my mom's nonstop berating us about what we'd done wrong, the pain we were causing her by answering the door, and then her lashing out, blaming others for her distress.

This happened so many times that I learned to block a lot of it out. However, what I came to know was that the most my parents could ever stay at a church was two years, as my mother would make sure to coach my father, manipulate his perspective, and completely sabotage his relationship at the church. She would spend a lot of time manipulating him, forcing him to request a move. At that point the church members would typically be ready for us to leave. This happened within so many churches that Dad got a reputation as a problem pastor. I cannot understand why he would not just stand up to her and tell her he'd made the decisions about his own career. If he or anyone else stood up to her, there was a shift in her eyes and tone, an immediate lashing out that twisted the truth and adapted the narrative: she'd make the story a complete circle, which started with our departure as her idea, then it changed to our idea, where we were the problems who had forced the decision. I did not know as a teen that this was manipulation, and my questioning my own memory was part of the gaslighting.

In an era before cell phones, my mom had her own ways of keeping tabs on me. She'd had an eating disorder throughout my life—in fact, so much so that my dad asked me to monitor her eating, including her binging and purging pattern. Looking back, I recognize that I should have never been put in that position, where I would report on mom's behavior whenever he returned from work or temporary duty. Well, I do not think my father realized how this put me in the spotlight, making me the problem child in mom's eyes. There were many times when I would report the behaviors I'd observed, and my mom would tell me she knew I was a "tattletale" and that I should not forget to "run and tell Daddy." I have vivid memories of watching her behaviors and reporting them to Dad, then of Mom and Dad fighting, Mom saying I was lying, and Dad believing her. I just wanted to please my dad, but there was always a catch. Eventually, this pattern stopped, but as I got older, their attention shifted onto me and what I was doing. Mom would monitor my eating habits, exercise routine, and interactions with others. She projected her own eating disorder onto me, telling others that I was anorexic and to watch me at school. One day I remember Mom fixing a huge breakfast and requiring me to eat it. I was so full that I could not eat lunch at school. I did get juice and milk—but no food. When I returned home from school, I walked into the kitchen, and Mom immediately said, "So, you did not eat at school today?" I was dumbfounded, and not knowing what to say, I said, "I ate a little." It was a lie but, I knew the wrath I would get. She knew I had not eaten, because she had secretly asked a friend of mine to watch me and report back to her. I felt as if I had no moment to be myself and I had no power over my life. This also occurred around the time her control over the relationships I had with my dad, sister, brothers, and other family members worsened.

I knew from at least the age of 12 that I had to make a plan to get out of my environment. I would visualize myself going to college and having a career, but first, I had to get be old enough to learn to drive and then get a job. I wanted more for my life than getting up, going to school, studying, and coming home. I was a good student and knew in my heart that education was my way out. I had to learn how to outmanipulate the manipulator because there were limited ways to beat my mom at her own game. I had to learn to predict, think ahead, and walk on eggshells. I often felt as if I had to go even further in predicting her next move, thinking ahead to where the eggshells were being placed so I could figure out how to navigate the fragile eggshells (my mom) so they would not crack.

Fast-forward to when I the legal age to drive and was learning on a standard ignition. I was not good at it, but I managed. I was determined to learn how to drive so I could gain independence in my life. There were limited opportunities to practice, but I did it when I could. Our other vehicle was an old brown Dodge Caravan, an automatic, and I drove it occasionally, even using it to get my license. My memories surrounding these events are scattered, as there were problems with friends and dating and, more painfully, the ostracization combined with the triangulation between my dad, sister, and me. There were so many dark moments that led to my own severe depression, often causing me to stay in my room, crying, with suicidal thoughts. I remember thinking how miserable life was while trying to gather my strength to push forward. As an adult, I now know it was my own resilience and spiritual beliefs that pushed me forward.

My mom would try to manage "my bad mood" by using her cosmetology skills. She'd gone back to school when I was in middle school to earn her cosmetology degree. She used my sister and I to experiment with haircuts, hair coloring, and hair styles, and she would often say, "Girls, it's time to do hair." There was no option to decline her offer, because if we did, my dad demanded we obey. There were times my hair almost fell out due to over coloring, perms, and many more experiments, and there were haircuts that were either not in style or were exactly like my mother's style, all of which led to my own personal hell. Already depressed, I would look at my hair in the mirror and cry. There was so much emotional pain wrapped up in my hair, making bullying at school common; it was obvious to me that my mother wanted to make us girls unattractive. She would demand that she do our hair, and if we acted like we did not like our style, it became our fault for not sitting still or for wanting something done that would ruin our hair. It was never her fault, never due to her behavior. I remember the many times I would sit in her "chair" and say, "Only a trim, Mom." I'd feel a cut and then, suddenly, I'd have a very short and unattractive cut. As I'd jump up, she'd say, "Well, I have to finish it now." This went on until I was 16 and no longer allowed her to touch my hair. She was furious and laid on the guilt, even getting my dad involved, but at that point, I refused. She then had to find other ways to control me.

The summer before I entered 11th grade, my depression was finally lifting, but Dad had served two years at his church, and it was now time to move. I remember standing in the kitchen of our old parsonage, looking out the window alongside my sister, distracted; I was telling myself that things would be different with this move. Boy, was I right and wrong. I was tired of the facades, the control, and feeling like a stranger in my own home. I did not feel like this was my family. My sister had just graduated from high school, and I could not understand why she'd not moved out. I would have been gone. My dad barely spoke to or acknowledged me, my sister was preoccupied with her new boyfriend, and I was just trying to survive. We got everything packed for the move. As we were pulling out of the driveway of the parsonage, I sat in the back seat, watching from the back window, feeling hopeful for new opportunities.

Moving during the summer was ideal because I'd gotten my driver's license and was determined to find ways to gain my independence. I would graduate in two years, and I needed to do everything to save my money and get good grades to prep for college; I'd start as soon as we'd moved into the new parsonage and settled. I remember asking my mom to take my sister and I out to look for jobs. Of course, my mom found her way to twist it, saying, "I will take you both out to look for a job—but only if you get one today." And I was determined to make it happen. As we drove around putting applications in, she reiterated that if I got a job, I would have to find a way to and from work or to pay her for gas. I reiterated to her that I would do whatever I needed to do. My sister wanted to do the search alone, but I wanted to go as well. I knew my future, and it involved making money. We spent the afternoon looking, and I felt confident that I would get a job, even though I had no real reason to feel hopeful. My final stop, Chick-fil-A, felt promising. I completed the application, turned it in, and the manager asked to talk with me. The conversation went well, and he told me he would let me know by phone if I got the job. I walked to my mom's car with a smile. My sister seemed furious at my smile and said, "You will only get it because you are thin and pretty." I just accepted the comment, but I'd never thought that about myself. In fact, I was very insecure since I'd had a bad breakup and faced years of bullying, weight fluctuation, and hair disasters, all leading to my lack of self-esteem. I let it go because my focus was on work, and it was only a couple of days before I intercepted the phone call at home, grabbing the phone before my mom could answer. The call was from the manager at Chick-fil-A, who offered me a part-time job on nights and weekends.

I started my junior year at a new school and focused on academics, work, and completing my studies. This kept me away from home and the chaos, but not all of it. I did manage to meet a great guy, and he is now my husband of over 30 years. When he first asked me out on a date, I was reluctant to accept, as I'd been heartbroken from a previous relationship and knew how embarrassing my family was—and challenging to manage. I remember telling him, "I don't know. I will think about it. Plus, my mom will not likely let me go out with you." I said this as I was walking out the door, leaving work. I then opened my mom's car door, as she'd come to pick me up. When he asked again later, I said yes, but I knew I would have to go home and directly tell my mom and dad that I would be going on a date and be picked up on Friday night. I knew my mom so well that if my date were to just show up, she would play nice and not say anything to make her look bad. I was right, but my dad tried to act like the caring and protective father, which came across as quite silly to me. But my date said it was an intimidation tactic. I had not been protected in my childhood, so I wondered, Why now? I found out that Dad had been told to act that way by my mother.

My boyfriend, now husband, has been with me through so many things in my life. It is quite hard to consider how much he sacrificed to stand by me through it all—so many horrific things Mom did and Dad defended. There are too many to mention, but some include the times my parents told folks, even my teachers and friends, that he was a drug addict; when they attempted to portray him and his family as trashy; and when Mom would tell lies about my father, sister, brothers, grandparents, aunts, and the friends in my circle. She wanted to get him on her side, to sabotage our relationship, and to make him so paranoid and worried that he would be drawn to her, not his family. This worked until we were able to figure it out, but we did not see my in-laws for a couple of years as a result. I regret it to this day, and it's painful to admit.

When we started dating, we were inseparable. Our relationship got closer, and he would drive me to and from work for months, until he eventually asked his parents for permission to sell me his older car and that he could buy another one. He sold it to me for very cheap—my first car, a Chevy Cavalier. I could use it to drive to and from school and work. It felt good to have a job, my own money, and transportation. Of course, my mother attempted to poke holes in all of my new independence: the car, dating, working, and school. She demanded that I break up with him, which I resisted. She even made up a story, saying I was attracted to my sister's boyfriend to cause a rift between my sister and me, which worked. There was never a dull moment, even when I desperately wished for some calm.

The story of my sister, her pregnancy, and her boyfriend got twisted to the point where I was told to move out of my own bedroom and to "find a place to live." We had a screaming match, and my sister accused me of wanting her to abort her child, hollering about how I wanted to be with her boyfriend. In reality, her boyfriend had confided in me about my sister's behavior and asked for my advice. When it came to my sister's pregnancy, I was disappointed only because I'd hoped she would go to college instead of get pregnant in the first place. Of course, my intentions were twisted into something more sinister, portraying me as a horrible sister. This led to two incidents that my mom still denies happened. First, I was kicked out of my house and had to stay with my boyfriend's parents, who would drive me to school every day to save gas money. Second, once my sister had her baby, I was never allowed to touch, comfort, or play with my niece. My mom and sister were the only two allowed to engage with her. It was heartbreaking, as I wanted to be a part of her life. My return home after the birth was just as abrupt as my departure. I remember coming back to my boyfriend's house after work. It was an era prior to cell phones, and his mom, who'd just gotten off the phone, said, "Your mom called, and she said you had to come home tomorrow." My heart went into my chest. I laid in bed that night, thinking about how I could survive being back home. I just had to finish high school (I would finish in the top 20) and carry out my many positive future plans.

Over the years I was in and out of contact with my mother. Sometimes, I'd take a break because I needed space from the lies, abuse, and pain. Other times, she would call me and make up some story about how I'd ruined her and my dad's life in some way. I shed far too many tears while thinking I was the problem, and I felt so much guilt without truly understanding why. I'd lost my identity, even though I'd typically followed most of her demands. I abided by them, which included paying for my own clothes and graduating from high school. I followed her demands for limiting contact with specific friends and family, for my wedding plans, for visits with her and my dad, but I resisted them regarding where I went to college.

No woman in my family had gone to college before me, and I was determined to go where I wanted. I step back now and ask myself why I complied, and you are likely wondering that too. Well, there'd been years of being brainwashed by her love bombing and gaslighting, years full of fear of her retaliation, her manipulation, her blaming me for her pain, and her reminding me of all she'd done for me by birthing me and providing a roof over my head. I lived the reality that I had no right to be happy, to make my own choices, or to be independent of her. Mom constantly reminded that she was the only one who truly loved me but would pair it with all my faults and the ways I'd hurt and disappointed her. How did I disappoint her? By moving out to get married, going to college (not the one she wanted), traveling, attempting contact with my siblings, and enjoying time with my friends and in-laws. All of this led to my screwed-up self-perception, which led me to engage in other highly controlling relationships, especially with women. Moreover, I had an unhealthy attachment style (anxious and avoidant), was afraid to have my own children, had cut out the healthy people in my life, was passive, had difficulty making decisions, never trusted others, and always overanalyzed everything.

I would love to say that counseling saved me. In some ways it did, but it was mostly the support of my husband and children and the discovery of my own tools, which I describe in this book. From training to be a counselor, I learned to look at what my life experiences have taught me. First, they've made me resilient and strong; they've reminded me that I have a spirit that pushes onward and upward. Overanalyzing is a gift as well. I have a very high intuition that I have learned to listen to and can use as a counselor, mother, and friend. But I've also learned to turn it off for my own sanity. These tools have helped me survive and make decisions about managing my relationships with my parents, siblings, family, and friends. All these experiences led to my choice to go no contact with my mother and father. I finally learned that my experiences were not unique. In fact, many folks have experienced a caregiver/parent, partner, colleague, friend, or acquaintance with narcissism. The impact on me and others takes a lifetime of healing, but this book can hopefully make a healing dent in those shattered parts of yourself.

Reflecting upon my history, I wonder when I decided that I would one day pursue a career in counseling. I instinctively knew I must work on myself before I could help someone else, but when I was growing up, I could not go to a counselor—or even ask—because it would have been denied. I'd heard folks in my family say far too often that crazy folks went to Whitfield, which I later learned is a state mental health hospital. As I headed off to college, I struggled a lot to manage the varied things in my life, and I found I thought quite a lot about my experience of sexual abuse, which finally led me to pursuing counseling. My very first counselor was a social worker, and she was very impactful in helping me process my sexual abuse and the apathy of my family, who had not intervened or reported the abuse.

As I progressed in school, I earned an associate degree and then a bachelor's in sociology. After graduation I examined options for my master's degree and determined that my local university had an accredited counseling program. Counseling programs encourage that all counselors in training do "their own work," which led to me pursuing additional counseling. It has often been asked, Who helps the helper? Well, there are many folks who can help the future counselor, psychologist, and social worker.

As I pursued counseling, I found that while I was telling my story of sexual abuse, I really wanted to focus on my family dynamics, which extended beyond the sexual abuse story. Yet I found I was being asked to rehash this story over and again, to have a narrow focus, when I was internally seeking to understand the bigger picture of why I felt so disconnected with myself, so guilty for no reason, so perfectionistic, and why I could never seem to live up to the expectations of others. When I explored this with counselors, most would talk about boundaries and forgiveness, but they offered no real help with providing skills to manage these feelings or to understand what I was experiencing. The forgiveness therapy aspect was good up to a point, but it was based on the assumption that I'd had varied events in my life that I needed to forgive people for so that I could let go of any resentment or pain. This was supposed to provide a sense of relief. The idea was that if I forgave, this would create a new and healthy relationship with my parents. I did almost all that I was asked to do in counseling, but I was quite frustrated that there was an assumption that forgiveness was the only answer. I could forgive them but still face lasting problems that need to be addressed. As a result of being in and out of counseling that offered varying advice, I stayed connected with my family, but they kept up the same behaviors toward me, and I would just take it from them and question what I'd done wrong. No matter how much I agreed with them, acted passively, tried to please, and put up boundaries, there was never a time with a sense of peace. Chaos always resulted, along with lying, manipulating, gaslighting. They continued evoking their will upon me, which led to my own confusion, emotional turmoil, and guilt. It had taken me so long to finally talk to a professional about my family dynamics, as I was embarrassed and hid the stories until I was an adult. To feel as if I were the one who had to solve it was exhausting. The problem is that there were very limited solutions, so I knew I had to do something different. I was not cognizant of exactly what that could be, but I'd continue to delve deeper, looking. Then events began to unfold that heightened my awareness.

I grew up as a Christian. Even when my parents didn't attend church, I always had a strong faith. It was tested when I was sexually abused, as my uncle was very involved in the church and his behavior had seemed to be condoned by everyone. I remember laying on the ground, looking up at the sky, and asking God why he would let this happen to me. As an adult, I know that it was not God but my uncle's free will that allowed it—but it was very painful. With age and experience, I developed my relationship with God and went to multiple churches with my husband; I even worked in a church for a while, seeking to find my place and my calling. I knew I did believe in God and that I wanted to help other people, to try to live according to moral and ethical principles, but I was in search of my spiritual home.

I attended several Christian churches that ranged from very conservative to more liberal ideals, but nothing felt right for me. I have a sense of the eternal, and I feel it resonates within me, but no doctrine has fit within that framework for me. It was not until I was sitting in a session with a client in 2015 that I was introduced to a new spiritual practice. This client was practicing a prayer method, exploring his own belief system, and the principles intrigued me. As I delved into this concept—the readings, principles, and meditations—I finally felt a sense of peace and unity, and my empathy expanded, teaching me to not only have empathy for others but for myself as well. I found my home as a spiritual being who is worthy of being loved and is loved by a higher power: God. Additionally, there came a sense of calm and relief with focusing on personal prayer, mindfulness, journaling, reflecting, and enhancing my intuition and spirituality. These principles and practices began to help me feel empowered to love myself just as I had loved others, as well as to listen to my intuition. I continue to practice some of these principles, along with others, which I share in this book as a healing tool. Once I had a spiritual connection in my life that fit, I approached counseling experiences or interactions I had with a much bolder perspective and clearer sense of purpose. It was after about a year of this practice that I finally felt empowered enough to confront my mother. I knew I may not get the result I wanted, but I had to do it and to decide to go partial or no contact. Honestly, I was hoping for the best but expecting the worst. It was far worse than I imagined. However, for once in my life, I was prepared. I was devastated at first, and it took me a long time to process what had happened, my choices, and to consider a no-contact future.

In the midst of this journey, I continued to be a professor and to have a private practice, where I worked with varied clients who were experiencing a range of mental health conditions, including a history of narcissistic abuse. When individuals are exposed to abusive and nonvalidating environments, it is highly likely they will develop depression, anxiety, and/or even personality disorders. One of the personality disorders I found myself working with was borderline personality disorder (BPD). I did not feel adequately trained to assist those with this disorder, but then, through a supervisee I was working with, an opportunity to become trained in the number one evidence-based therapy for BPD, dialectical behavioral therapy, presented itself. This training, which took place in California for two weeks and which I fit in between work, changed my perspective as a counselor and abuse survivor. Exposure to this theory validated my spiritual walk, provided tools that could be of use to me, and reinforced that I mattered and that my healing mattered.

As I walk through each moment, each day, each experience, and each interaction, I seek to walk in a perspective of taking each moment as it comes. I combine the use of my spiritual beliefs, my intuition, and a combination of varied theories of psychology as a lens for my own healing. Of course, I utilize my years as a counselor and educator, as well as my personal experiences and the support of my immediate family, to navigate the new me that has been unfolding. There will always be more to learn, but I've been finally moving into my authentic self.

I am hopeful that having a glimpse into parts of my life helps you to see the importance of recognizing that narcissistic abuse is real. All individuals exposed to this personality disorder will have varied experiences and choose different paths, whether these are full contact, superficial contact (partial contact), or no contact. It can take a lot to make this decision, and the tools provided in this book are a step toward achieving the choice that is right for you. Please take a moment to reflect upon your own experience as either the direct recipient of or as the observer of narcissistic abuse.

Reflective Journaling

What experiences in your life story influence your decision-making (e.g., childhood, friends, family, education, work, faith, etc.)?

_____

_____

_____

What strengths have you gained from these varied experiences throughout your life?

_____

_____

_____

What personal responses do you need to be aware of as you engage with other individuals/acquaintances at home, school, work, etc.?

_____

_____

_____

CHAPTER 2

~

Narcissistic Personality Disorder at a Glance

Over the last 10 years, the term "narcissist" has been discussed in social circles, with the label of "narcissistic" given to those who are self-focused, egotistical, controlling, and abusive. The term has been thrown around often, making it difficult to render a true diagnosis of narcissistic personality disorder (NPD). It is critical that, before we delve into the healing process, we delineate the difference between what is a personal versus a clinical perspective of someone who falls within the characteristics of NPD. We ask, how is an individual diagnosed with this disorder? Once we understand the characteristics of someone with NPD, we can see the trickle-down effect that someone with this disorder has upon the people in their life, including partners, family members, coworkers, organizations, and larger systems. To defeat the giant and recognize the impact of NPD, we must first understand what contributes to the diagnosis, how it is recognized, and the characteristics that are evident, as well as how narcissists view the world and how they engage with others.

Diagnosing Narcissistic Personality Disorder (NPD)

The *Diagnostic and Statistical Manual of Mental Disorders* has been around since 1952 and is now on its fifth edition, with a revision having recently been introduced (2022). The manual covers a range of diagnoses, with hundreds of mental health disorders listed, each one outlining criteria using signs and symptoms that must be met; each one also has a specific International Classification of Diseases code for billing purposes (American Psychiatric Association [APA], 2022). The professionals you may seek out for help are required to take a diagnosis course in order to have an overview of the diagnosing process. To get an accurate diagnosis, they utilize assessments to adequately diagnose clients and to reduce the likelihood of bias, which could lead to a misdiagnosis. As a licensed professional counselor, I am aware of the requirement for healthcare practitioners to adhere to the ethical standards promoting the appropriate use of assessments with clients (American Counseling Association [ACA], 2014). I know you, the readers of this book, have likely been diagnosed with a medical or mental health condition, or you know someone who has. Thus, you are aware of the process it is to diagnose conditions when you or someone you know goes to the doctor.

Pause for a minute, and consider your initial reaction when you sought help due to exposure to someone with NPD. You can go to the end of this chapter and jot some notes down from these questions, or you can ponder these in your thoughts. Is there a sense of fear that you will be misunderstood or that the clinician might think you are blaming someone else for your problems? Would your NPD partner never allow you to go to treatment without them, and if they were to come to a session with you, would the helping professional be easily manipulated and side with the NPD abuser? Are you so broken that you do not even know where to begin when talking to the helping professional, as it all seems surreal or unbelievable?

If so, you are not alone, and you have chosen the right book to help you. Before we can get into ways to heal, we do need to briefly touch on the diagnostic criteria of narcissistic personality disorder so you are fully aware of the traits and the behaviors that are commonly attributed to someone with NPD.

Let's get a bit technical for a few minutes. According to *DSM-5TR* (2022), NPD is characterized by a grandiose sense of self-importance, fantasies of power, the idea of being special, exhibiting greedy behaviors, envying others, a sense of entitlement, mood shifts when not at the center of attention, manipulation, and a lack of empathy for others. Although it is more commonly associated with narcissistic grandiosity, NPD can also include vulnerability characteristics as well (APA, 2022; Stanton & Zimmerman, 2018). Delving further into the actual criteria within the manual, we find there are specific criteria that must be met within each category. A person must demonstrate or report significant impairment in their ability to function because of their personality, which is referred to as impairment in self-functioning either specific to identity or self-direction (APA, 2022). Let's break it down. Under the component specific to identity, a person with NPD might rely on others to help define themselves. Specifically, they are seeking self-esteem and/or identity but with a measure of self that is either self-inflated or -deflated, and it can even go back and forth between the two. Under self-direction, all goals and standards are based upon the ability to be noticed as exceptional by others, even if they are not consciously aware of this need, making it hard for them to notice the motivation, except that they feel a sense of entitlement (APA, 2022). The other criteria fall within the impairments of interpersonal functioning in empathy and/or intimacy. Counselors are taught a lot about the importance of empathy in the helping profession, but with individuals who have a NPD, there is an impairment with their ability to be empathetic. They can be empathetic when what they say or do is self-relevant, but they lack insight into how this lack of empathy impacts others around them. Their intimacy is quite superficial and is maintained for their own personal gain, fed by the personal desire to promote their own self-importance and self-esteem (APA, 2022). We can imagine that some of our relationships are more intimate than others due to our level of connection with the person. And some relationships are meant to be more intimate. But an NPD individual's relationships are used as a means to an end, for their attention seeking and for promoting their personal needs and drives.

Have you ever heard of the word psychopathology? NPD individuals have pathological traits that greatly impact those around them. The first is grandiosity, where the level of entitlement and their belief that they are better than others is so great that they use overt and covert means to maintain that grandiosity, which even includes demeaning others. The second trait is attention seeking, where they will do almost anything to attract attention and to be admired by others. I am sure you are pondering your own experience. You might have worked hard to graduate with your bachelor's degree only to be overshadowed by the behavior and conflict generated by your abuser on the day of graduation. They might have downplayed your success, working hard to get all eyes on the shining star, themselves: the narcissist.

As a result, it is important to remember that with these traits, they must be consistently expressed across multiple situations over time to receive a diagnosis. I am sure that in your experience, these traits have been evident across many different areas of life. Also, their personality impairment cannot be justified based upon development (APA, 2022). Think about a teenager who is seeking to solidify his or her identity and is worried about what peers think. This is normal for development for a teenager, but when an adult consistently has this need, it can be not only as a red flag but also quite embarrassing to those within their circle. Some might ask, Could the problem be something other than NPD? Well, yes. Before diagnosing anyone, clinicians will make sure this client's personality impairment is not due to a medical condition, use of drugs or medication, or head injury. All of these characteristics explored in the diagnostic manual may add up to an individual potentially meeting the criteria for a diagnosis of NPD; these individuals have characteristics that are quite harmful to others since an excessive need for admiration is evident at any cost. Add the lack of empathy, manipulation, and remorse. Although the *DSM-5 TR* does not have additional subcategories to what has described so far, there are professionals who've explored additional nuances surrounding narcissism. You can merely search the internet, and you will see information emerge regarding the potential for anywhere from three to ten types of narcissists. I think this is because their behavior crosses all aspects of one's life and can be detrimental. But it can be hard to keep up with what is scientifically proven versus the information others share based upon their experience with a narcissist. I will address what I have seen in my practice to provide context beyond the *DSM-5 TR*, which focuses on grandiose and vulnerable/covert narcissism.

I have seen malignant narcissists, who are very malicious and aggressive and who gain pleasure by seeing or inflicting pain, whether that be physical or emotional. Overt narcissists are very aligned to what is described in the *DSM5-TR* (APA, 2022) as grandiose narcissism, except these individuals are preoccupied with how others see them. There is a high focus on status, wealth, flattery, and power. Covert narcissism is also referred to as vulnerable narcissism, as discussed earlier. This type is a subtler form of NPD, as these individuals are very sensitive to criticism, envious, and self-serving, and at times, they can seem shy and withdrawn while still exhibiting some destructive behaviors, such as gaslighting and passive-aggressive communication. We explore what gaslighting is later, as well as break down the varied communications styles. When we consider the characteristics of this diagnosis, we find that those with NPD follow a recipe of sorts to have an impact on folks in their path.

If someone you care about or know has some traits of NPD, it can be challenging and even impossible to get these folks to come in for mental health treatment. If they do, helping professionals cannot diagnose this disorder based solely upon clinical judgment, but they must rather rely upon some form of a test to measure certain characteristics of the client. These are often called assessments and are used to make informed decisions. The Narcissistic Personality Inventory (Raskin & Hall, 1979) and the Minnesota Multiphasic Personality Inventory (Butcher et al., 1989) have been used to measure narcissism. Of course, there are free quizzes and assessments online that are easily accessible, but they may not have any research behind them to support the given diagnosis. Just like with a medical diagnosis, we want someone who has training and uses the correct diagnostic tools to make an accurate diagnosis, not unlike how we'd want an MRI to diagnose a tumor.

When we are living with or interacting with someone with narcissistic traits, it can feel as if our whole lives are intertwined with their abuse, so we ponder if this is normal, and if it is, how common NPD is. In a study conducted within the United States between 2004 and 2005 with over 34,000 individuals (about twice the seating capacity of Madison Square Garden), the prevalence rate of NPD was only a little over 6%. Let that sink into your mind for a minute. If you consider 34,000 individuals, the diagnosis of NPD would account for roughly just a bit over 2,000 of them—that is, it is not as common as one might think. However, for those who experience NPD within family systems, the far-reaching impact for such a small percentage of the population is enormous, especially since a common characteristic of NPD is a lack of empathy. If someone is lacking empathy, what are the typical ramifications of that person's behavior? If you let your mind wander over the layers of impact, you might find that thought too emotionally overwhelming. Now that we have explored how a clinician might diagnose NPD, let's explore the practical characteristics you likely experience daily when exposed to someone with NPD.

Practical Characteristics of Narcissistic Personality Disorder (NPD)

Over the years many self-help books have emerged to assist children, partners, and agencies in understanding the practical aspects of NPD, along with how to heal after being caught in the warpath of someone with this diagnosis. It is important to understand that there are likely many individuals with NPD walking around, undiagnosed, so it behooves us all to be able to recognize the practical characteristics should we find ourselves sitting across from an undiagnosed (or diagnosed!) narcissist at work, in a social situation, or even in a relationship. As a licensed professional counselor, I know when a client sits across from me, it is important to provide space for them to share their story. Anytime people share something that has happened, they are sharing through their lens, their perspective. It might be quite easy for someone with little or no experience with NPD to listen to the experiences of someone exposed to NPD and chalk those up to exaggerations, old age, cognitive distortion, or just plain untruths. In reality, for those who've been in a relationship with a person with NPD, the truth is often worse than anyone can imagine. Take a deep breath before you delve into reading these characteristics listed on Textbox 2.1. I hope that reviewing this list will help to validate your experience.

TEXTBOX 2.1. CHARACTERISTICS OF NPD

- Lying, manipulation, selfishness, blaming, projecting, dramatic, chronic self-pity, disparaging others
- Love bombing to draw a partner into a relationship, and when the relationship shows the potential of ending, using loving behaviors to draw the person back into the relationship
- Destruction of relationships within families, communities, peers, and systems
- Pathetic attempts at helplessness when confronted with behaviors
- Lack of awareness of others' feelings; lack of empathy
- Blames others for their problems or for the behaviors the individual with NPD actually did
- Never admits to being wrong; an apology may be used as a manipulative tool
- Projects their own flaws or deficits, such as problematic behaviors and motivations, onto others (e.g., declares that a coworker is trying to manipulate their boss when it is actually the individual with NPD doing this)
- Exploitative for own self-interest and gain
- Parentification used as a form of control to transfer what they are responsible for onto others with no consideration of others' needs
- Aggressiveness and childlike behavior utilized to meet own needs
- Use of fear, lying, and ruthless behavior to terrorize/control others
- Defensive when criticized by others but quick to criticize others
- Selfish, willful, and manipulative of others' emotions, with enjoyment of others' pain to feed his or her ego
- A need to be the center of attention; might rob others of the spotlight
- Gaslighting to make others question their memory (gaslighting is when a person with NPD manipulates a person to make them question their perception of reality)
  - Example: You remember the narcissist telling you something over dinner, but the next day, they deny it was ever said
  - Example: You were cursed at and slapped by your abuser, but the next day you are told you were too intoxicated to remember and it did not happen, even though you have a mark
- Denies, excuses, and justifies behaviors toward others as necessary for his or her "own good"
- Violates boundaries due to feeling as if "What is yours is mine"; takes on the right to define others' needs and interests

- Favoritism is evident between family members, coworkers, peers, and friends
- Minimizes others' accomplishments using tried-and-true tools to undermine the significance of life events

Many clients I have worked who've been exposed to NPD commonly ask, "Why can't all counselors recognize an NPD abuser?" I have pondered this, journaled about it, asked fellow clinicians, watched clinical tapes, supervised trainees, and thought about my own experiences to answer this question. There are a few reasons I have found from my years of clinical experience that explain why the traits of someone with narcissism could be missed. First, narcissists can be excellent manipulators, and counselors, who are human (just as their clients), are taught to see the best in all people; thus, they do not assume someone is lying or manipulating. It can be easy to miss the signs until the lying, manipulation, and/or aggression is directed toward the counselor. Second, if someone with NPD comes to a session, it is quite common for that person to come in alone, not bringing other family members, and to convey stories about family that encourage the counselor to side with the narcissist. In other words, the NPD person paints a very negative picture of others within their lives. Unless the counselor obtains permission to speak to other family members through a release of information (or there is a legal requirement to do so as a result of a client revealing suicidal or homicidal ideations), the counselor receives only a skewed view of the events being portrayed. Also, counselors are ethically required to work with the identified client, which, in this case, is the individual with NPD. Finally, if the NPD person is a partner, a parent, or even an employer, they can present as very confident and competent in a counseling session, even making the counselor think that the NPD person has the best interests of others in mind; the counselor might believe the narcissist's warnings to not trust the other person (e.g., partner, child, employee), and thus the narcissist has created a sense of bias in the counselor before they ever see the other parties. NPD individuals will commonly come to counseling alone or request to talk to the counselor first, before the professional works with the other family members or parties. If a partner, child, or employee comes in with the NPD individual, they may be very fearful to speak up due to the wrath that follows when they do, or the NPD individual may do all the talking. I find it necessary to shed light on what I've seen in counseling treatments when an NPD abuser takes the lead in a session. It is important you understand that I have a keen eye for manipulation, having come from my own history with

NPD abuse. If a clinician is reading this, I am hopeful their ears will perk up and they will notice the patterns in these interactions we now explore.

Counselor-Client Interaction: The Conversation With Someone With NPD

I had a client who was new to my caseload, and all I was told was that this person was presenting to treatment for help with family problems. Family issues are a common reason to seek out a counselor, and I have worked with many similar client cases before, so there was an expectation that it would be an easy intake and treatment planning process. Reflect on the characteristics of someone with NPD as you read through the following interaction:

The First Session

I go over the informed consent and ask if there are any questions. The client immediately lets me know that her background is in nursing, and therefore, she knows all about informed consent and confidentiality and that there was nothing I shared she did not know already.

The main question she asks is about my background. The person immediately asks, "How long have you been doing this? Can you work with people with issues like ours?" I am a bit taken aback at the questions, and I feel the need to defend my education, background, and skills. Once I can move on from the informed consent, I let her know that an intake is required and that I will be asking many questions, seeking information about the client's history of mental health, medical concerns, family dynamics, and so forth.

The client stops me and, through tears, says, "I just am going to tell you straight up that I am here because of what my spouse and children have done to me."

So I empathetically say, "I can see that you are tearing up as we begin this intake; it sounds like there are a lot of difficult experiences you need to share today."

The client quickly responds, "You better believe it!" And the tears quickly stop.

A commentary about the interaction is as follows: As the intake proceeds, I ask questions about what brought the client to counseling and about her mental health history, medication, current and past family dynamics, trauma history, education, employment, substance use, children, and treatment history. I am attuning to her as I hear about the traumatic experiences this client has been through—the level of verbal, emotional, and financial abuse at the hands of her partner and children, as well as how being an ethical nurse has led to her unemployment because she's stood up for what is right amid nurses that "wouldn't do their job." I affirm the client's strength for coming to counseling, enduring these difficulties, and for her stellar work as a nurse.

The client replies, "Thank you, I am so glad you understand."

Here is my commentary about this interaction thus far: The client feels very validated and heard, but as I go into developing treatment goals, the client quickly indicates that there is nothing wrong with her parenting style, communication, or relationships, but rather it is her children and partner who need to be seen. There is a quick transition to her discussing that her attendance in counseling today was to make sure that I was a good fit for the needs of the family and to check my credentials for adequately working with them.

She explains, "I am not here for me, because I am fine. I really came to make sure you are a good fit for my family. They must be fixed."

I respond, "I need to remind you that you are considered the identified client."

A commentary about her comment is as follows: I remind her that she is the identified client, not the other family members. This sparks anger and frustration within the client.

She angrily spouts, "Well, I am not the problem, my family is. They treat me horribly—they use, abuse, and take advantage of me. I am the smartest person in my family, yet they treat me like I am stupid and don't listen to me. You need to do something about them. I plan to go home and tell them to come to counseling because you affirmed how abusive they are."

Here is my commentary about her comments: Based upon counselors' abilities to tune in to the behaviors being exhibited, they will have varied reactions. As an NPD survivor, I have heard and experienced this type of interaction before, but it is possible that a clinician, not unlike me, might have to sit and reflect a minute. It would not be uncommon to not be sure of what to say or how best to proceed, and they might quickly defend the perspective of the person who is the identified client and their role.

So what might happen?

A first possible response might be as follows: if I say, "I cannot ethically treat your family members without getting their consent and obtaining their story," the NPD client could potentially make me look like the crazy one by saying, "Oh, really! You just told me how abusive they are to me, so why do you need approval to see them? You need to be reported." She might attempt to manipulate my perspective by telling me a story about how one of the children treated her over the last week.

A second possibility is that if I stand my ground ethically, there is a likelihood this person will go the pathetic route and say, "You are the only one I have ever told this to, and now you are treating me like they do. Can't you just help me or find someone who can?" All of these comments are said in an attempt to get me to do what she wants, no questions asked. If I do not give in, the client might come back one more time, but more than likely, she will tell me how unprofessional, uneducated, and unskilled I am and that she needs to talk to my boss or be given another counselor. Also, she may never return to counseling again after sounding off a defensive and insensitive response to my decision.

A third option becomes possible if I were to consider seeing the partner or children just once. The NPD client might indicate that she will schedule the next session for the other party(ies), but unknown to me, she has no intention to "let" me have a session without her present, even if I were to assume that the session would be with the partner and/or children. The spouse or children would not be allowed to see me alone, even if it's just to complete an intake with them and get their side of the story. The NPD client wants to control the narrative, so solo sessions are unlikely. If I am not careful, I could get trapped in a narcissistic web of lies.

Realistically, how would a counselor know they were trapped? I cannot speak for other clinicians, but it does take experience and a willingness to listen to behaviors and watch for cues to not get trapped in the web. I would stick to my ethics, reinforcing that this person is the identified client and the only way I would see the whole family is if I could get each person's perspective individually. You are likely thinking, if only my NPD abuser could be required to go to counseling or to get tested! But I know it is rare for someone with NPD to attend treatment.

I have indicated how someone diagnosed with NPD might present in treatment, but since they do not commonly attend counseling (unless it is required in some way or it is to manipulate/persuade a counselor to work with another family member who "has the problems"), it is essential for a counselor to consider how a someone might present in treatment after being exposed to a partner, parent, legal guardian, or supervisors with NPD and are in need of help. In these scenarios, it is likely you might see a glimpse of yourself and remember your experiences with a NPD abuser.

Throughout my career I have worked with children, teens, and adults. I remember when I first started out as a counselor, it was not easy to spot someone who'd been exposed to NPD abuse. It was particularly challenging to spot an NPD parent, especially among those bringing in their child or teen for treatment. However, I got better at seeing the signs that go along with the symptoms described by the parents.

Practical Characteristics of a Client Exposed to NPD Abuse

Child

Reflect upon your childhood experiences. Most individuals can remember their best childhood memory and the worst. Unfortunately, for children with NPD parent/guardians(s), there are most likely many difficult childhood memories to convey. From my experiences both personally and professionally, I've found not all children are given a voice in their home. Due to the age of consent to treatment in most states ranging from 16 to 18, children and teens are commonly brought to treatment by a parent or legal guardian. The informed consent process (ACA, 2014) typically involves the parent(s), child, and counselor. All parties need to sign off on the treatment of the child to ensure that legal custody is explored, there are limits to confidentiality, the client is identified, and all parties sign the document. When I'm working with children, my typical pattern is to ensure that the parent(s) and child were in the room during informed consent and to begin the process of completing the child intake. It is common to ask developmental, education, medical, mood, and behavioral-problem questions to the identified legal guardian. I typically get that basic information from the legal guardian and then ask the legal guardian to leave so that I can speak with the child or teen alone. Over time I have found that with an NPD guardian (typically one parent), they start off like any other parent. They give details about the questions posed, but when those questions lead into the child's emotions and behaviors, the NPD parent is unlikely to take responsibility for contributing to any of the behaviors acted out or emotions experienced by the child.

See, for example, this interaction from when a mother brought in her kindergartener for behavioral problems at home. The mother says, "I do not know why he acts this way; I have done everything the books say regarding behavior management, and he is still bad and spiteful. He seems to do these things on purpose just to hurt me, and I will not put up with it. I do not want you meeting alone with him, because he is just going to lie, manipulate, and tell you I am mean to him. I am a great parent, and I will not stand for you two ganging up on me. If it is going to be that way, I will go to another counselor."

Meanwhile, the child has his head down and is silently playing with a toy in my office.

This parent is setting the stage to let me know that I will not meet with the child alone, that the parent calls the shots, and that the child is somehow miraculously past the developmental age of a kindergartener and is purposefully manipulating everyone. When this happens, I remind the parent that the client is the child and it is important to meet with the child alone, that there will be times with both the child and the parent(s), but not always together. My experience is that the child will express very little in the session, whether I meet with the client alone or with the parent. It is quite unlikely that the child would speak up, give an opinion, or show autonomy in any way, as the NPD parent has controlled, brainwashed, and told the child that they have no voice. If their voice is expressed, there are tools used by the NPD legal guardian to mute the child's voice and opinion. This creates a child who has difficulty with attaching to the caregiver or other adults and who is likely going to constantly seek love and approval from that parent. Do you see yourself or someone you love through the lens of this child? I encourage you to go to a journal and reflect upon this perspective. What does it mean to not have a voice? What does it mean to have a voice?

What if I agree to the parent's terms? What if I indicate how my ethical responsibility is to make sure the child can express himself, especially if the parent is reporting behavior problems? If I agree to the parent's terms of only meeting with the parent and child together, I will get reports of the child's poor behavior at home and school, as well as of methods of punishment that have isolated the child "for their own good" until they can "act right."

An intuitive counselor would want to talk to the other parent (the non-NPD one) and maybe even would seek to obtain a release of information so they can talk to the school, teachers, and other caregivers to explore what is happening in the other settings. What makes this very difficult is that there are no obvious signs of physical abuse; however, there can be clear signs that this child is emotionally withdrawn—for example, maybe they present as a "little adult," not a child who is exploring their world. Once the mother catches wind of your interest to inquire of others, expanding beyond her controlled circle, the child will likely not return to counseling anymore. Some might ask, Why would the NPD legal guardian bring this child to counseling in the first place? As the reader, I am sure you may have even been that child in the seat. The parent wants to be seen as the doting, educated, smart, superb, and selfless parent of an ungrateful and terrible child. They feel the need to spend the time letting the counselor know how well they are doing and how horrible the child is behaving, as well as that nothing the counselor is doing is working.

Teenager

Will the NPD parent act differently if it is a teenager coming into the session? Well, yes and no. I've seen some of these teens present very differently. On the one hand, by the time I've seen some of them in my office, they'd already been in juvenile detention several times—possibly in acute care or maybe even long-term care for their behavior. I am not saying that all teens who have been in these facilities have NPD parents or guardians, but some of them do. I have worked with many teens, and sometimes, by the time I get them in my office, they are completely withdrawn and angry at the world but also fiercely independent. As a teen, I was very independent but very suspicious of adults. I am sure you can relate to this perspective.

For example, a parent entering a session with their teen may say, "I do not know why she has such a smart mouth. I do everything for her, yet she disrespects me by staying up late, telling people I am mean to her, and not following the rules. I can't believe they say she is good at school. She is manipulating those teachers because she is horrible at home. She is acting all innocent now in front of you. Of course."

In response, the teen may be sitting in the chair, looking down at her phone, and not saying anything. She may even be thinking, "I made my mom and dad mad, so I needed to be sent away."

The parent may continue, "All she does is rebel, curse, lie, and sneak out of our house—that I pay for."

Here is my commentary regarding these comments: the parent quickly replies to get control of the session and let me know the teen is the problem. I've had the opportunity to get some of these teens signed up for services in the presence of the parent, but due to their juvenile incarceration or lack of school attendance, I could also see the teens alone. Some of these kids, the ones raised by NPD legal guardians, explained how the constant parental control led to their rebellion, as they felt nothing they did was right in the eyes of the parent. The teens chose to act up because nothing they did, whether it was good or bad, made a difference. The legal guardian would typically tell everyone how horribly the teen behaves, reporting all sorts of problems to medical doctors, teachers, and anyone who would listen—all while the teen sits nearby, slumped in a chair. When I would get teens alone in a session, I would find out that they wanted the trajectory of their life to lead them out of their home and the controlling environment.

I feel like I must set a caveat that there are some teens who are physically aggressive, violent, and even purposely work to make the parent(s) upset. It could be linked to many different things, such as mental health, genetics, environmental factors, use of drugs, and/or gang involvement, and there are other predictive factors (Lawrence & Nkoane, 2020). I have worked with a wide range of clients with other problems. However, it is important to note that Barnert et al. (2021) reinforced that teens with parental problems, which one could easily include an NPD parent, are at higher risk for incarceration. Thus, all of us who have been exposed to NPD as a child or teen can be at a higher risk for emotional and behavioral problems due to home-life history and exposure to NPD abuse. This can carry over with us into adulthood.

However, some teens of NPD parents are not rebellious. I've worked with teens who wanted counseling. This might have been sparked due to their threatening suicide or a traumatic event, or it may have been ordered by a court due to divorce. Some of these teens have commonly talked about how they just can't seem to make anyone happy, especially their legal guardian. They present in treatment as being the sole problem in their family; they take responsibility for divorces and caregiver happiness; and they feel an escape from life, through suicide, would be better. The guardians of these types of kids have commonly talked about how the teens' problems were taking an emotional toll on them, the guardians. They once again blame the teen for hurting them psychologically, then reiterate how the teen's problems caused them distress. When I was a teen, my mom would tell other people that my behavior was "breaking her heart." All I was doing was going to school, my job after that, and then back home and repeating the cycle. That accusation of causing a parent pain can be very difficult for a teen to understand.

What is the common element so far? The guardians explain any problems with their child or teen in a way that leaves space only for how they are impacted, not the child. The guardian presents and believes they personally have no flaws and that they parent effectively and have given the child or teen the best life, that the child or teen owes them their life, and that the teen must live and act within the confines of what is expected by the NPD guardian. The child or teen is seen as an extension of the guardian, causing pressure for perfection. As you read through this, can you picture yourself in this scenario? Were you or someone you know in a far worse situation? Consider your experience of counseling or lack of counseling and how that has shaped you.

Unfortunately, my clinical experience has shown me that most clinicians miss the signs of a child or teen who's been exposed to an abusive guardian with NPD. As a result, eventually the children grow up with varied problems that might lead to their seeking counseling. To understand this, we need to explore a bit about attachment and maternal deprivation studies, which we do in a later chapter. As an overall summary, children with NPD parents do not typically have healthy attachment patterns and thus have a difficult time with understanding themselves, accepting self-love and love from others, and demonstrating an ability to accept or understand emotions; they also have chronic personal disapproval, a lack of unconditional self-love, and other acceptance issues due to a lack of trust. Additionally, there may be a broad spectrum of people-pleasing tendencies that encourage them to act at their own expense or be fiercely independent. Since I have explored how a client with NPD may behave in treatment as well as how a child and/or teen exposed to NPD abuse may present, there remains a need to explore what the relationship might look like for an adult relationship impacted by NPD abuse.

Partner, Colleague, or Supervisor: NPD Adult Relationships

I've had a lot of experience working with adult survivors of NPD abuse. I have worked with clients both while they are still with their partner and after they are no longer with the person. I have also worked with individuals who work in an environment where an individual with NPD is either a colleague or a supervisor, and in treatment, they often report having been bullied, ostracized, and trapped in their environment. Common characteristics of an adult who is surviving or has survived NPD abuse include loss of identity, loss of self-esteem, self-blaming, being driven by guilt and fear, expressions of shame, self-disapproval, lack of self-acceptance, questioning of their memory, inability to trust others, and being withdrawn from life. Stop reading, and think about these for a minute. Consider if any of these resonate with you.

I remember one client who came to me; she was feeling so disconnected from herself and others. Prior to her seeing me, she'd canceled her first appointment. This is not atypical, as it is hard to reach out for help and trust someone. When we finally met, she presented in this way.

Sitting with her head down, in a quiet voice, she expressed her reason for being in counseling: "I do not know who I am anymore."

I replied, "Please elaborate a bit more for me so I can understand better."

She said, "Everything in my life was centered around my partner, and now that he has left me, I am nothing."

I sat quietly for a few seconds and took it all in.

A commentary of the interaction is as follows: at first thought, I considered the grieving process of the relationship, which is natural, but as the session unfolded, it became clear that her partner had made her an extension of him. She spoke of herself in very self-deprecating ways, saying things like "I am not that smart—he was the smart one"; "I really liked for him to make decisions about everything, it made him happy"; and "He is right, I can't do anything without him."

Here is my commentary on her comments: I do not judge her perceptions, but I want to focus on the importance of her identity, decision-making, and self-perception. These may seem like subtle statements, but as we progressed in treatment, I found that there had been many years of NPD abuse by her father and then her partner. This cycle of choosing individuals with NPD characteristics is common for abuse survivors when it comes to choosing a partner or a friend.

What does this look like within you? You might be very driven and potentially guarded, but you are likely resilient. However, behind your wall of strength, you might be hiding a sense of shame and the feeling of being disconnected and alone while lacking the ability to make decisions. Adults who've been exposed to those with NPD may commonly be diagnosed with anxiety, depression, and PTSD, and some may even develop NPD as well, as they were exposed during their formative developmental years.

Pause right here. I am not saying you have or even will develop NPD. I know this is a big fear that folks exposed to NPD abuse have. Here it is very important to mention attachment. Bowlby (1969), Ainsworth, and Bell (1970), in their research with the parent-child relationship, reiterated the power of nurturing and caregiver responsiveness in influencing attachment patterns. I speak more about this later.

If you are told by the person with NPD that you are the problem, you are crazy, then you have been lied to and manipulated by the narcissist, have become their scapegoat for all their problems. Who are you to become once that relationship is over? Or if you were to be continually told this, what would happen to you if you could not escape? Adult survivors are not always disconnected from unhealthy environments; often, they are still knee deep in the same or similar experiences. In fact, for partners, colleagues, and subordinates, it is very challenging to get out of these relationships. Most of my clinical experience has been with women survivors of NPD, but we need to remember that both men and women can be NPD abusers. We often mistakenly assume that all survivors of NPD are women, but there are men surviving those relationships as well. Statistics do show that more men are diagnosed with NPD than women, but it is important to step away from any preconceived ideas about victims vs. abusers in order to work with anyone who presents as being exposed to NPD abuse.

Typically, these clients present with symptoms they identify as depression or anxiety. I remember one man indicated that he'd just come out of a long relationship and expressed that he'd "lost himself," finding himself "unable to get out of bed," "unmotivated," and "lost," without the ability to have joy in life or make decisions that benefited him. Just recently, I was approached by a woman at a prominent institution who reported that a female colleague had sent her degrading, unprofessional, and blaming emails daily, while her boss indicated that she should just be "ignoring the emails" versus taking action to stop the harassment. As a result, the woman questioned herself and her own emotions. Imagine if it is your supervisor who you want to please. They remind you that your job is always on the cusp of going away, that there is an expectation of meeting the supervisor's need, and you may be exposed to frequent yelling and degrading episodes. There may be many days when the victim would prefer to avoid work.

Even with these symptoms present, it may be difficult to pinpoint someone who is exposed to a partner with NPD. It is imperative to do a thorough biopsychosocial assessment/intake and really delve into the dynamics of this person across all the domains of their life, which includes their family, work, education, and community involvement. The realization of the impact of NPD on this client might only come several sessions later.

When delving into these discussions with the client, I find it is not uncommon to hear the client say, "I really had problems with coworkers. I think there is something wrong with me. I do not know who I am, I cannot trust myself, my memory, my thoughts, and I feel unlovable/misunderstood."

This statement is just one of many red flags that may indicate an unhealthy relationship pattern or interaction. In a later chapter, we explore strategies to help you heal, but it is important to consider how recognizing characteristics of NPD abuse survivors impacts not only your view of self but your view of the world and, thus, your engagement with others.

NPD Survivors' Worldview and Interaction

Survivors of NPD present in different ways for treatment based on their age; however, they commonly have various ways of perceiving themselves and the world. As indicated earlier, we have a hard time accepting ourselves and trusting the world around us. Why? The experience of living with a person with NPD has taught us that both trusting others and being in relationships are not safe. Whenever we have trusted someone, especially someone we care about, we have been hurt tremendously by the problems they've blamed on us, the receiver of the abuse.

Consider the metaphor of swimming far out, taking a risk, and then the tide comes in. A tide will take you in or take you under, requiring you to seek a new strategy to survive. Just when a survivor thinks he or she is making headway, the tide (like an individual with NPD) takes over, and the survivor is swept up, damaged. The damage is immediate, then terminal—just as you would imagine happens with drowning in deep water. What is an NPD survivor drowning from? Everything! The survivor's sense of identity and loss of self, the sense of self-blame they feel for their predicament, their low self-esteem, and the inability to trust their own ideas, values, and intuition. Years of exposure to an NPD abuser creates a barrier with trust, developing an insecure attachment pattern, where the victim's reality is that of not feeling safe around others. This leads to their suppression of feelings and people-pleasing acts, leading to unhealthy relationship patterns. They lack assertive communication, the capacity to express their needs and wants and trust in their own decisions. This creates an individual who wants to hide from the world, literally and figuratively. Consider a child, teen, or adult who pulls away from attention, realizing that getting attention leads to problems. They have learned it is more important to make sure that others are okay, while the survivor's needs are not important—thus, people-pleasing at all costs. To avoid engaging with others, it is common for an individual to avoid school, work, and engaging with friends, and they often have difficulty in social, peer, and romantic relationships.

Considering your age as a survivor reading this book, you might find it quite difficult to recognize the problem, as the environment in which you live seems normal to you. A child survivor might be very quiet in the presence of peers, in the classroom, or with other adults, and they will commonly seek to please others no matter the cost, even at the expense of their own safety. Consider how you interact with family members, peers, teachers, strangers, and friends. It is usual for survivors of NPD abuse to have a small circle of friends, have some paranoia about the intentions of others, and to have limited interactions with others, except when approval is provided by the person with NPD. When I was a child, I was not allowed to have guests over or spend the night with friends; I had limited interaction in social activities, and my parents spoke for me. An adolescent who's been exposed to NPD might become an overachiever and never miss school due to not wanting to be at home; they might go to school, then work after school, and constantly pursue a way to stay active and busy. Sometimes, this is for their own self-preservation, or it's due to a requirement to be responsible for others in their family, whether that's to meet their own basic needs and wants or those of their parents/guardians or siblings. Adult survivors who've been intertwined in an NPD relationship will slowly start losing their assertive voice and will commonly do what their NPD abuser requires of them. It is common for an NPD person to seek out a people-pleasing individual who will not buck their requirements, making folks with a history of abuse a prime target. If a survivor's perspective bucks their requirements and they have an assertive personality, the relationship will likely not last. It is not uncommon for a person with NPD to be married multiple times. A survivor recalls that the person they were prior to meeting the narcissist is not the same. They report feeling damaged. Depending upon when the NPD exposure began and how long it's continued, there might be a culmination of multiple symptoms reported.

I appreciate you hanging in there as we've explored varied facets of NPD. The diagnostic (*DSM-5 TR*; APA, 2022) characteristics of NPD have been explored. After reviewing the characteristics, I am hopeful that I've provided a glimpse into how the NPD survivor experiences the abuse and what results. After reviewing the characteristics from varied perspectives, we've explored real-life cases and how we all might manage this. From their exposure to NPD, the victim/survivor finds their worldview shaped by the abuser; this dictates a path that might seem very hard to navigate, but there is the possibility to heal and be their authentic self. We delve into the power of attachment in the next chapter.

Reflective Journaling

After reading this chapter, reflect on your experience with someone with an NPD diagnosis.

_____

_____

_____

What has your experience been? Are you a survivor of NPD abuse? Or have you been around someone who has been exposed to NPD abuse?

_____

_____

_____

Consider your personal and professional strengths. What can you draw upon as a means of managing your own exposure or when engaging with someone with NPD?

_____

_____

_____

CHAPTER 3

~

The Power of Attachment Patterns

When someone announces they are expecting a child, there can be a range of emotions. However, we typically show expressions of excitement, joy, and wonder at bringing a new life into the world. Of course, there are expected and unexpected pregnancies and varied reactions to hearing the news based on the parents' worldview. Depending upon one's culture, it can be quite common for folks to believe that the ability to nurture a child comes naturally to parents. As helping professionals, we know that parenting and the response to a child is, in fact, very challenging, and it is very common for a child to be raised in a similar way to how the parent was raised. Alternatively, someone can also make a conscious effort to do the opposite of their caregivers from their childhood. We need to get the myth out of our head that bonding, attachment, and relationships between the parent/caregiver and child are natural and easy. Why do we need to explore this? It is important because survivors of NPD abuse are influenced by childhood attachment patterns. These patterns influence how we relate to parents, peers, friends, romantic partners, and other relationships. In this chapter we explore a broad overview of maternal deprivation and attachment theory, attachment styles, and how these styles impact the child, possibly perpetuating an unhealthy allegiance to the NPD abuser.

Caregiver Deprivation and Attachment

To understand the impact of exposure to NPD abuse, we need to look closely at survivor/victim children as they grow into adults and observe what that exposure can lead to. The very act of labeling a caregiver as depriving may conjure up many images of abuse. I do think it is important to break down

41

the two words. The definition of a caregiver is someone who looks after a child or a sick or elderly person to ensure all needs are met (American Psychological Association [APA], 2023). Deprivation is defined as lacking the basic needs of life (APA, 2018). When the two words are put together, they indicate that a child fails to thrive due to some form of neglect from the caregiver, but the type of neglect is not mentioned. Is it physical or emotional? As you think back regarding your own story, reflect about your experience with your caregivers.

Consider the conception and birth of a child. The expecting parent feels a range of emotions. Those who give birth to the child often feel a greater level of responsibility for this life; further, there is a general perception of their greater role and responsibility. A baby's behaviors includes crying, whining, kicking, and finding any way to get their caregiver's attention. What does an infant need? Food, shelter, protection, attention, a feeling of safety, and to have their overall needs met. Babies often have different kinds of cries: one for food, another for a diaper change, and others for comfort, swaddling, and reassurance. The caregiver is instrumental to the child not only getting these needs met but with the child's knowing they are protected from danger. The caregiver models love. Consider this: the child cries and the caregiver responds. However, what happens if the child cries and there is no response? Of course, a caregiver may be delayed in their response, but typically, there is a response. There are some folks who believe in allowing babies to "cry it out" because, to them, the child needs to learn to sleep through the night and to not always get their needs met immediately. Of course, there is debate for and against this parenting style, but this is different from deprivation. In a depriving environment, the child may not have been fed, dressed, changed, rocked, spoken to or nurtured in any way. The child's screams may get louder and louder but then more faint. The child realizes no one is coming. Think about what that teaches the child about the caregiver. Remember, we know most children get what they need to thrive and survive. You and I are living examples of surviving whatever circumstances we were exposed to as an infant. Sometimes, we may say to ourselves, "Well, I am alive, so it must not have been too bad." But isn't there more to being alive than just living? Yes! There's love, a feeling of belonging, security, and passing on the skills that promote nurturing, love, and healthy relationships.

Mary Ainsworth conducted research she called the "strange situation," which reinforced how powerful a mother is in shaping child's view of the world as an infant and how that influences the future. Mary Ainsworth's purpose for this experiment to observe how attached a child is to their caregiver. She hypothesized that the way a mother (caregiver) responds to the needs of the child between the ages of 9 to 18 months influences the attachment pattern of the child into adulthood. She did this by observing the behavior of the infant child across eight different scenarios lasting 3 minutes each. It started with the mother, baby, and Ainsworth (a stranger) standing alone in a room for less than one minute. Then, the next scenario put the mother and baby alone in the room, with stranger then joining the mother and the infant. On the fourth step, the mother leaves the baby and the stranger alone, and then the mother returns and the stranger leaves. After that, the mother leaves, and the infant is left completely alone until the stranger returns. The final step sees the mother return and the stranger leave. From her observations, Ainsworth developed the attachment styles, which were mainly based on what she'd observed when the mother returned to the infant and the stranger left, then when the stranger returned and the mother left. There were behaviors that were specifically reviewed and tracked. Mary Ainsworth viewed proximity and contact and watched for behavior indicating whether the infant did or didn't want to be near to or seek out the caregiver. Within the category called *contact maintaining*, Ainsworth (1964) focused on the observations around whether the child did or did not maintain contact with the caregiver (Ainsworth et al., 1978). From these situations and observations, Ainsworth aligned the infant responses to three patterns of behavior: secure or insecure attachment or insecure-ambivalent/resistant behavior. Secure behaviors were demonstrated in infants that missed the parent upon separation, would greet the parent when they returned, and then would reengage in play at that point. With insecure-avoidant behaviors, the child demonstrated little to no distress at separation from the caregiver, avoiding or ignoring the caregiver upon their return into the room where the child was playing. With insecure-ambivalent/resistant behaviors, the infant demonstrated high levels of distress when separated from their caregiver and sought out that connection and caregiver reunion, but they did not get settled by the caregiver's return and even were resistant to them (Ainsworth, 1964; Ainsworth et al., 1978). To paraphrase, according to Ainsworth, how an infant responds to the caregiver determines the category of the varied attachment patterns she'd identified (Ainsworth, 1964; Ainsworth et al. 1978).

Another name aligned to caregiver deprivation was given by John Bowlby (1958;1969), who worked with children labeled as lacking affection and even as delinquent. His original work explored the link between maternal care and mental health for those children who'd been institutionalized or in foster care most of their lives. He felt the distance between a mother and child's relationship is critical. The mother's choices, mental health, and lack of connection to the infant could lead to a child having many mental health problems. This might include difficulty with relating to others, resulting in shallow relationships, poor choice making and impulse control, and perpetual patterns of relationship dysfunction.

A marked finding from Bowlby's work that is significant to understanding your exposure to NPD abuse lies in how these children may be brought up with a caregiver who has a difficult time seeing a child as separate from themselves; they can almost see the child as a little adult when, in fact, the child needs a caregiver's skills to maintain physiological, emotional, and psychological well-being (Bowlby et al., 1956). Harlow (1958) studied early bonds as well. Harlow wanted to know how bonds emerge and how bonding—or a lack of it—might impact behavior and functioning. Bowlby went on to accomplish this through a test he conducted on rhesus monkeys. These monkeys were separated from their birth mothers and reared by surrogate wire mothers. The infants were placed in cages with two wire-monkey "mothers." One of the wire monkeys held a bottle from which the infant monkey could obtain nourishment, while the other wire monkey was covered with a soft terry cloth. While the infant monkeys would go to the wire mother to obtain food, they spent most of their days with the soft cloth mother. When frightened, the baby monkeys would turn to their cloth-covered mother for comfort and security. Harlow's work supported Bowlby's theory, which reinforced that the caregiver's role is important in attachment and is specific to comfort and care, extending beyond the role of feeding (Harlow, 1958). Consider what influences attachment: the opportunity to make attachments and the quality of the caregiving. The attachment pattern begins within all of us in infancy, and we continue that pattern unknowingly until it is pointed out to us. The nature of the attachment can lead to future unhealthy relationship choices.

For this book, it is important to break down the types of attachment styles that John Bowlby (1969) determined from his research. Review Table 3.1, in which we explore how attachment influences the impact NPD abuse had on you as a child as well as how you may be prone to continued abuse by others due to this attachment pattern. This is essential for the process of healing. In other words, being deprived of what is needed for a secure attachment pattern can increase our likelihood to connect with and choose the wrong people in our lives, and it can keep us locked within relationships where NPD abuse is common, for this is expected by the child victim who then grows into an adult. As you review these attachment styles, please take note of the attachment style and characteristics, and take an honest assessment of your own style. It helps to think back on how you've interacted with others due to your NPD exposure.

Table 3.1. Attachment Styles

Attachment Style	Characteristics
Secure Attachment	• This is the ideal attachment to enjoy healthy boundaries, intimacy, individuality, and social interaction. • This is developed by a child having caregivers who are positively attuned to the children, giving them attention, affection, and a sense of safety. • These children grow up to feel safe, trust others, and be emotionally resilient and regulated.
Insecure Attachment Styles:	
Ambivalent Attachment	• Caregivers are on-again, off-again, inconsistently tending to and attuning to the child. This creates doubt in the child that their needs will be met. The child is always on alert, looking for cues/clues for how to change their behavior to impact the parent's responses. • This leads to a tendency to grow up dissatisfied: they want love, but when they get it, they become unavailable due to a developed idea of "I can want love but cannot have it."
Avoidant Attachment	• Caregivers are emotionally unavailable, insensitive, and even hostile to a child's need for connection, so the child forms a coping strategy of disconnecting. • These children grow up lacking emotion due to lack of intimate nurturance. • The limbic system is impacted, with no signals for building relationships. • The adult develops a disconnection from others and believes they do not need others.
Disorganized Attachment	• Caregivers send double-binding messages to children. • The caregiver creates situations for the child that are unsolvable and unwinnable. • For example, the parent may express an idea of "Come here, but go away" or tell the child to do a task, then criticize them. • Parents are a source of fear for the child, yet they still desire their parents' love. • There is a conflict within: the children desire intimacy yet fear it.

The deprivation studies utilize these types of attachment to reiterate how insecure attachment patterns can lead to varied relationship problems. Thus, this pattern breeds an environment where it is easy to connect to someone diagnosed (or even undiagnosed) with NPD. This is particularly true for a child whose parent was diagnosed (or remained undiagnosed) with NPD.

When considering attachment styles that develop, we should go a bit further and explore adverse childhood experiences (ACEs), which contribute to problems with not only attachment but effective coping. Since NPD is a mental health disorder recognized in the *DSM-5 TR* (APA, 2022), exploring the adverse childhood experiences that lead to adult complications is important. According to the Centers for Disease Control and Prevention (CDC) over 60% of adults, report some type of ACEs associated with emotional, physical, and sexual abuse. They also report witnessing violence in a home, community, or school, along with unstable home economics within a family (Centers for Disease Control and Prevention [CDC], 2020). The original ACEs study and the subsequent follow-up studies suggest that these types of experiences can lead to various illnesses and even death. These include disruptions in neurodevelopment; social, emotional and cognitive impairment; engaging in risky behaviors; and mental and medical diseases. When broken down further, this includes traumatic brain injury; fractures and burns; depression; anxiety; suicidal ideation; potential PTSD; and chronic diseases, such as cancer, diabetes, and addiction, as well as overall worsened quality of life (CDC, 2022). Let's consider both attachment theory and ACEs to explore the potential consequences of exposure to an NPD parent and how that can then lead to an adult child of an NPD parent choosing relationships or environments that perpetuate this cycle. Textbox 3.1 outlines the impact of NPD exposure. Refer to the characteristics of NPD from Table 2.1 as you explore the impact further. As you read through this list, I encourage you engage the stop technique: stop and look away from the page, take a deep breath, observe your body sensations, and then proceed back to this section of the chapter.

TEXTBOX 3.1. IMPACT OF NPD EXPOSURE

- Chronic self-blame, shame, personal disapproval, and lack of acceptance
- Low self-esteem and belief that they are the problem
- Echoism (difficulty with voicing their own opinion, lack healthy narcissism (belief in self)
- People-pleasing with friends, family, peers, and coworkers
- Difficulty accepting praise
- Self-doubt, including minimization of skills
- Loss of identity, purpose, and meaning in life
- Repressed feelings
- Insecure attachment with others with potential for unhealthy bonding
- Caretaker of others at the expense of self

- Develop fierce independence and refusal to ask for help
- Do not trust other people, especially those who are the same gender or in the same role as the abuser
- Do not trust self to make decisions
- Overthink the behavioral intentions of others
- Question their memory about events
- Organize life around happiness of persons with NPD and others
- Unhealthy relationship patterns, including the potential to choose controlling friends and/or partners
- Poor communication patterns
- Conflict avoidant
- Hypervigilant responses to situations
- Psychosomatic symptoms
- Mental health disorder

When looking at the list above, perhaps you can clearly identify aspects of yourself. However, it is essential to break this down a bit further so there is a broader perspective on how parenting style, bonding, and subsequent development of insecure attachment patterns influence and impact day-to-day life. Hopefully, by exploring each of these, we can begin to set the stage for honoring the reality of your experience.

Chronic Self-Blame

It is not uncommon to hear a survivor say that it is their fault when something goes wrong. They might think they've not listened well enough, not been attentive enough, or been absentminded, causing the NPD individual in their life to escalate. The survivor has learned to explain the abuse by believing they have done something to cause the problem. This is exactly what the narcissist wants their victim to do. When someone is told long enough that they are the problem, they easily walk away with deep feelings of shame. The survivor is always self-evaluating, identifying themselves as the problem, and living a life full of shame, lack of self-acceptance, self-disapproval, and a lack of trust in their own decisions.

As a counselor, I frequently find that survivors present with a passive communication pattern. When survivors inquire about symptoms, family patterns, and concerns, they commonly minimize their exposure to NPD and may not even recognize it as any form of abuse. They hold on to the clear perception that they are the primary problem, and they seek to figure out why they are "broken" and ask what needs "fixing?" A common statement

I hear is "I want to know what is wrong with me. I know I have a problem, but I am just not sure what it is." As the process unfolds, you begin to clearly understand how the NPD abuse pushed the survivor to not only accept the abuse but also the blame for it.

Low Self-Esteem

When someone has chronic self-blame, there is typically a link to low self-esteem, and they reiterate that they, not the NPD abuse, are the problem. This low self-esteem is often connected to their physical, emotional, psychological, academic, and other attributes, which likely have been attacked and blamed by the NPD abuser, reinforcing the victim's low self-esteem.

You may never think you are smart enough, good-looking enough, or capable of reaching your goals. You might have expended lots of effort to support the goals of the narcissist and not your own goals. You may lack a sense of your capabilities to achieve your own goals. These beliefs require you to seek a way to live with these flaws and accept that all humans are flawed. Sometimes, these survivors might seek counseling at the request of the NPD, who wants them "fixed." Also, friends or family member may see problems arising in survivors due to their lack of self-esteem (e.g., potential eating problems, weight problems, academic challenges, stopping and starting projects, lack self-motivation).

Echoism

This is a concept that is quite hard for us to wrap our minds around. When we think of an echo, we often think of standing in an empty auditorium, shouting, and then waiting for our echo to return to us. Echoism is a bit different, as it refers to an individual's struggle to express themselves. There is an underlying fear that others will perceive the person as too self-focused. According to Savery (2018),

> echoism is a condition, whose name derives from the Myth of Echo and Narcissus, in which a curse is placed upon Echo that stops her from having her own voice and forces her to repeat the words and thoughts of another as her own. In its clinical counterpart, the echoist, it creates a state of absence of being in which the individual foregoes being-for-herself in favour of the other, and is thereby reduced to a being who is barely alive and without agency or sense of self. (p. 154)

In other words, a person who demonstrates echoism lacks a healthy level of narcissism, or belief in self. We can believe in ourselves, have a healthy self-esteem, and be concerned about our own needs without being a narcissist. All of us should feel we have a right to be on the earth, to take up space, and to contribute to the world.

The individual will consider the needs of others way before considering their own needs. They worry they'll come across as needy, and they lack self-identity, except in relation to others. The echoist, derived from echoism, does not like to be the spotlight, has low self-esteem (explored earlier), put the needs of others first, might self-efface or self-deprecate, and does not ask for help while perceiving themselves as the problem.

People-Pleasing

We know and understand the concept of people-pleasing quite easily. We make sure that everyone around us is pleased with our decisions, which come in the form of behaviors. We see this behavior with parents, children/teens, siblings, teachers, students, coworkers, and in every walk of life. A people pleaser has a very strong urge to please others, even when it's at their own expense. It is not a formal diagnosis, but it can wreak havoc on an individual's life.

I call myself a recovering people pleaser. Upon meeting a people pleaser, you may find that the person comes across as passive, with their head and eyes down, and yet they are very observant—they're watching what you and others do so they can figure out how to please you. When you ask a pleaser to do something, they commonly answer yes, as they often find it very difficult to say no to others' requests. As a counselor, I find that when I ask a pleaser to do some absurd amount of clinical homework or to attend four sessions a week, they say yes, even though, in the back of their minds, they want to scream, "No, that is way too much!" In work settings these pleasers might talk about feeling overwhelmed, but it is likely due to their taking on extra work or projects to please a coworker or boss. In social activities or volunteering, this is the person who is overcommitted with lots of plans, responsibilities, and projects. Pleasers do not have the skills or healthy self-perception needed to advocate for their own needs and desires. They typically say, "I'm fine" when they are not, or "I'm sorry" when there is no reason to apologize. They find it nearly impossible to say no, since pleasers are the "yes" crew, and they only speak honestly or voice their opinion(s) when those ideas are rooted in others' wants (or what they think others want). So a pleaser will go along with decisions to avoid what they perceive as causing friction or a problem. Think of being asked about what you want to eat for dinner. A pleaser will typically wait for everyone else to decide. Or they may mention pasta, but the other person wants tacos, the people pleaser will switch and go for tacos, even if they are allergic to or cannot stand them.

What does this lead to? This opens the door for others to take advantage of you. It creates persistent unhealthy emotions, such as stress, which leads to anxiety. There is a lack of self-care and a potential for chronic low self-esteem, with an addition of huge conflict avoidance. Not all conflict is bad, but people pleasers perceive it as such. In reality, it is a critical tool to learn in life, especially when strategies for conflict management and resolution, which help people learn how to navigate conflict, are utilized (Rahim & Katz, 2019). People-pleasing can impact your life and interrupt daily living skills.

Difficulty Accepting Praise

Ask yourself, How do I respond to a compliment or praise? It can be hard to answer this, but it may include deflecting, minimizing, or discounting a verbal gesture that comes in the form of a compliment regarding some positive trait a person sees in you—for example, "You are such a wonderful chef." "I really like blue on you. It brings out your eyes." "You really are a talented artist."

Typically, if you struggle with accepting praise, you may deflect that compliment, thinking that your skill or behavior is not as good as that of someone else (e.g., your partner, coworker, or family member). If a boss were to recognize a strength within you, you might respond, "I just do what I need to do. There is nothing magical about me." This is a way you discount your ability to cope with or manage something. Sometimes, accepting praise is so challenging that a person might immediately reciprocate to get the focus—and thus the pressure—off of themselves. For example, they may respond, "You look so nice in your suit today." "Well, take a look at yourself, you always look fantastic."

Loss of Identity

With NPD exposure, a person may not only lose their identity, but they may not ever have the space to even develop a sense of identity. When examining the word *loss*, consider the concept of no longer having something. Now replace that something with identity. What would that be like? And why? Well, it might have been destroyed because it was not seen as meaningful or important. You may ask, To whom would it be important? Well, the narcissist. It would be quite common for someone struggling with identity to say, "I feel lost. I do not know who I am. I am not sure if I ever did." Or they might say, "I used to know who I was, but now I do not." They likely question everything about who they are, which can lead to their withdrawal, isolation, and feeling as a "nothing." I have seen it time and again in sessions with my clients.

Repressed Feelings

When someone represses their feelings, they are typically avoiding uncomfortable emotions. There is a tendency to push feelings down, which includes pushing memories out of their conscious awareness. Why? Because it is safer, and it helps them live daily life with less stress and worry, as feeling these emotions would bring unwelcome pain.

You might not be able to express many emotions while you're exploring your history of abuse, exposure to traumatic events, dysfunctional childhood, poor communication, and so on. In dysfunctional environments, children learn not how to communicate but to control their emotions. There is quite a bit of minimization of emotions, or saying things such as "I do not get angry."

Caretaker

The basic and historical definition of a caretaker describes someone who takes care of some kind of building or even of animals. In this context a caretaker is someone who cares for others, but this can include many different types of people and experiences. Typically, to be a caretaker is a choice someone makes, not something imposed upon them, but for folks exposed to NPD abuse, the role of caretaker is forced on them as a necessary skill for survival—to the detriment of their own self-care.

People pleasers might find themselves saying how much they like helping others, while, on the other hand, they might be frustrated by doing so much. They might understand at some level how much their identity is linked to being needed by others and the underlying reality that the role of caretaker is one of the few things they can control. Melody Beattie wrote extensively about individuals who allow another person's behavior to impact them. Thus, they lose themselves due to the extensive efforts they make to predict—and ultimately control—the outcome of another's behavior. This is referred to as codependency, and there are many varied ways to define a codependent person, but they face an obsessive need to caretake others at the expense of themselves while attempting to solve others' problems that are not their responsibility. This can look like desiring to rescue another person from themselves when it is not the people pleaser's / codependent's responsibility to do so (Beattie, 1992).

Fierce Independence

This can be hard to define, but we can understand it when we look through the lens of behavior and thoughts. Someone who is independent typically wants control over their own life. There is a focus on achieving individual choices and perspective without support or aid from others, because the person can do it independently. If we add the word "fierce," it makes us think of having an aggressive desire to achieve things alone, without the help of others.

If you are fiercely independent, you will commonly say you do not need anyone or that you are better off alone. You can be very successful due to your fierce independence, which has led to academic, employment, and relationship success. But you may not reach out for support, help, or solace when there is a clear need for support and help. You have likely found that asking for or needing help from others only leads to reliance and owing the person something—thus, problems. This is what you have learned from exposure to caregiver or adult NPD abuse.

Lack of Trust in Others

To understand what *lack* of trust is, we need to know what trust is. It is the belief that someone's truth is reliable and honest, which upholds the character, ability, and/or honesty of another. If someone lacks trust, they do not believe what they are told is honest, truthful, reliable, or credible, as they've had numerous experiences of dishonesty.

Most of the time, you may have no problem expressing that you do not trust others. You may be reluctant to share much, if any, of your life story with anyone until there trust is demonstrated and built over time. There might be a mistrust of specific types of people, a certain gender, or a particular stage in life. As time unfolds, it is quite common to not be able to trust specifically those who characteristically fit the image of your NPD abuser. You have been lied to, gaslit, and manipulated so much that you do not trust anyone.

Organize Life Around the Happiness of Others

This focuses more on an action rather than on a definition: when one organizes something, they place things in their proper place. But what does it mean to organize one's life around others? It means that survivor has placed things, including life events, out of their proper order: around what others' priorities, and not according to their own—namely, the NPD abuser is the priority, for survivor knows that if the narcissist is not, there will be consequences.

You are accustomed to the abuser being the center of attention, so it becomes quite natural to put your needs aside to serve the needs of the NPD abuser and what that person deems important in your life. This leads to a lack of healthy boundaries, as you focus on the needs of colleagues, partners, children, friends, and even bosses. You may say you prefer it this way because it makes you feel needed, and you may even acknowledge that this is what you are accustomed to doing.

Unhealthy Relationship Patterns

Due to exposure to NPD abuse, it is not uncommon for you to choose and stay with unhealthy people, whether they be intimate partners, friends, or work colleagues. All of these relationships perpetuate the cycle wo which you are accustomed, including poor communication and feeling unhappy, disrespected, controlled, and abused in varied ways, as well as feeling trapped, with no escape out of the relationship.

You might self-blame for all of the problems, minimize the unhealthy nature of your relationships, justify others' behaviors and your own response to those behaviors, and vacillate between wanting to move on but also fear leaving due to your desire to have some form of attachment to another, even if that is detrimental to your mental well-being.

Mental Health Disorder

Merely opening up the *DSM-5 TR* (APA, 2022) will show us that there is a plethora of mental health disorders you can develop due to genetics, environment, and ACEs. The mental disorders that emerge might include post-traumatic stress disorder (PTSD), depression, anxiety, or even another personality disorder (like NPD).

Realistically, you, the survivor, are more likely to come to counseling sessions than the NPD abuser. If you seek counseling, it is probably because you are in distress. It is not uncommon for NPD abuse survivors to have symptoms of depression and anxiety, relationship problems, mood fluctuations, a loss of identity, and suicidal thoughts. This are the times it is imperative that you take action to make a change. This book is an excellent step in beginning to change your life.

Unhealthy Allegiance to Abuser

Having read through the research on maternal deprivation studies, the attachment patterns in early childhood, and the impact of NPD exposure, I'd say it is quite easy to see why there might be an unhealthy allegiance to the NPD abuser. I consider the many years that NPD abuse survivors have been tangled in the narcissist's grasp. When a survivor is in an abusive relationship, whether that is with a parent, partner, or coworker, the abuser often resorts to behaviors that ensnare the survivors, keeping them tied to the narcissist. A person with NPD uses a pattern of manipulation to reinforce dichotomous thinking that divides folks into two categories: those who believe the narcissist and those who do not. If the person does not believe the narcissist, the narcissist will belittle and show favoritism to those who support them until the nonbeliever is broken into submission. Usually, manipulators wait until they're in a private setting to carry out behaviors that force submission, as getting the person aligned to the narcissist's point of view makes long-term submission easier. Soon after, the survivor is wearing the public persona that is all is well, which can go unrecognized to others, even professionals. The survivor might even dote on the NPD individual, upholding how smart, athletic, beautiful/handsome, wonderful, sacrificial, doting, and often misunderstood the person is if anyone were to see through the facade. These behaviors are evident whether or not someone sees through the allegiance to the NPD person.

Why do I call this allegiance? With allegiance, a person is committed to an individual, group, or a cause without questioning intentions or agendas. When someone does not have a sense of self-identity, as they've adopted the identity laid out for them by the NPD abuser, they exhibit an unhealthy level of allegiance, where things are not questioned. Think about that. Most folks will question some form of authority at some point as a part of figuring out what they can get away with, figuring out their ideas or identity, and finding out if there are potential problems, to name a few. Unhealthy allegiance makes it very difficult to pull away from an abusive relationship because the survivor fears lacking loyalty. Let's do a quick breakdown of what behaviors are evident with unhealthy allegiance and why its nature is unhealthy. You can review these behaviors in Table 3.2. This might be another good time to do the STOP technique. Stop and look away from the page, take a deep belly breath, observe your body sensations, and then proceed back to this table review.

After reading through this table, do you find you resonate with any of the problems noted on the list? What problems are not listed on Table 3.2 that

Table 3.2. Behaviors Resulting From NPD Exposure

Behavior of the Victim/Survivor	Problems That Might Arise in the Victim/Survivor
Never questions authority	Blindly follows instructions, even if personally or professionally detrimental
Dotes on the person	Loses a sense of their own identity and accomplishments
Defends the person	Takes away the reality that we all have flaws and should take responsibility for our own actions, that no one is perfect
Believes all the NPD stories, ideas, and plans	The person's identity, beliefs, and knowledge are all linked to the individual with NPD with no room for their own; they are 100% aligned to the NPD abuser
Minimizes the abuse	The person justifies the abusive behavior, explaining it is due to the narcissist's poor upbringing; likely feels they deserve the withholding of love, affection, attention, and/or the silent treatment due to their own mistakes toward the individual with NPD

you find are very important to express? Please use the blank journal lines below to assist you with this reflection.

Reflective Journaling

We have now explored maternal deprivation, the power of the caregiver, and attachment, and you can see how powerful the relationship with your caregiver is—how much it influences your future interactions. It is important to examine all factors, whether they include having a narcissistic caregiver or having an insecure attachment pattern. Both may have led to an unknowing NPD interaction. As we delve into the next chapter, I provide a self-assessment to affirm your exposure to a NPD abuser.

_____

_____

_____

_____

CHAPTER 4

~

Healing

Finding MEANING From the
Experience and Fostering a New Life

We explored my own journey with NPD and navigating the beginning of healing process. Like with a flesh wound, even when something heals internally, there are scars left behind—and they will always be there. The exposure to NPD abuse is one scar that is permanently there, a reminder left on the heart, mind, and spirit. It can be quite challenging to determine if you are in an NPD relationship or environment when it is all you know. For this chapter consider the use of a self-assessment as one tool for evaluating if you or someone you know is (or has been) in a narcissistic relationship. Assessment is powerful, as it provides a place to begin the healing process, but each person must do the work. I have found it helpful to create acronyms as a guide. For this chapter, we will explore the acronym MEANING. By breaking down what each of these letters means, we review what needs to be addressed and their accompanying action steps. You will learn how to M, master the art of self-love; E, express emotions in a healthy way; A, be assertive regarding emotions and needs; N, begin to develop a new identity; I, learn to live with intention according to personal values; N, begin the process of being the new you and living a new life; and finally, G, grieve what you did not receive from the NPD abuser.

The first step is to confirm that you have been exposed to someone with NPD. This can be a parent/guardian, coworker, family member, colleague, or acquaintance in your life. As you have read so far, it can be blindsiding to come to terms with the abuse. You have likely been convinced that you are the problem, or you may find it hard to explain how the exposure to this person has impacted you. To help make sense of the relationship, please look at the Narcissistic Exposure Quiz below. After reading each question, you will choose either yes or no for an answer. If you answer yes to multiple questions, there is the potential you've been exposed to NPD abuse. Even if you do not have many questions where you've selected yes, you may still need to continue exploring the skills provided in this chapter for treating exposure to NPD abuse. A yes to any of these questions offers important self-reflection for you or someone else, and the tools in this book can be helpful.

Narcissistic Exposure Quiz

Please choose "Yes" or "No" to the following questions:

1. ___Yes ____No: Were you quickly, after meeting this person, told by them that they love/like you more than others? Did they offer gifts and/ or provide praise, affection, or even say you are their soulmate or best friend?
2. ___Yes ___No: Have you caught this person telling others (e.g., coworkers, friends, children, family members, strangers) a lie about themselves or about you, but then they denied it when confronted?
3. ____Yes ___No: Have you been placed in a triangle in relationships that has led to problems where you are seen as the party at fault?
4. ___ Yes ___ No: Do you doubt your memory, the unfolding of events, or do you question your version of events in relation to the relationship?
5. ___Yes ___No: Do you seem to be the one who is considered to have the problem, which is reinforced by the inclusion of a third party?
6. ___Yes ___No: Do you often get the silent treatment when you're unsure of what you'd done wrong but know that you are being punished?
7. ___Yes ___ No: Do you often get told or feel as though you are the cause of the problems in your relationship?
8. ___Yes ___ No: Do you often feel as though you leave a conversation unsure of what has unfolded due to the lack of communication? You are not sure what you did right or wrong.
9. ___Yes ___No: Do you commonly catch your partner, significant other, colleague, or acquaintance in lies? This might include lying about whom they are hanging out with or what they are doing, or there is this person explains away the behavior to distract from the lies.
10. ___Yes ___No: Do you find yourself at the center of a smear campaign that discredits your character, which causes harm to and/or ruins your reputation?

11. ___Yes ___ No: Do you find yourself feeling very guilty but are unsure of what you have done wrong?

12. ___Yes ___No: Do you change your interactions, conversations, plans, and decisions due to being ostracized as punishment for your choices?

13. ___Yes ___No: Do you find yourself having physiological symptoms such as headaches, physical pains, blood pressure difficulties, and even digestion upsets due to the level of stress in the relationship?

14. ___Yes ___No: Do you notice that you are indecisive when asked to make decisions unless your partner or person of significance is there to provide feedback about the decision?

15. ___Yes ___No: Do you find yourself putting the needs of others as a top priority while forgetting about your own personal needs?

16. ___Yes ___No: Do you find it difficult to establish and then maintain boundaries with this person or others due to feeling you have no right to set boundaries due to your own lack of self-belief?

17. ___Yes ___No: Do you have moments of feeling very distressed, anxious, fearful, and unsure of how to proceed with your interactions with this person or others?

18. ___Yes ___No: Do you find yourself feeling very restless, on edge, nervous, and uneasy even when you are not around the person that triggers it?

19. ___Yes ___No: Do you find yourself doubting your judgment regarding future relationships and keeping folks at arm's length?

20. ___Yes ___No: Do you tend to not trust yourself and have difficulty determining and meeting your own needs?

21. ___Yes ___No: Do you find yourself wanting to avoid others due to being uneasy about how to engage with them for fear of causing problems?

22. ___Yes ___No: Do you find yourself experiencing a sense of identity confusion, forgetting your passions, skills, interests, and personality style?

23. ___Yes ___No: Do you attempt to leave the relationship but are sucked back in with promises to change, excessive gift giving, or temporary behavior changes?

After completing this quiz, stop and tally up how many yes and no responses you had, and write them down. Then take an extra step, and take 5 minutes to journal which of the yes and no answers were surprising to you. Next, write down your emotional reaction to your responses to these questions. Emotions are felt in different places in your body, but many individuals talk about feeling them within their stomach, chest, or even their face. After you have written down your emotional response, shift to your thoughts, and write down what comes into your mind. I call this head to heart and heart to head. Sometimes, we need to shift to broaden our awareness in the moment. Please start writing below, and then review Textbox 4.1 to see the breakdown of how this chapter can help you with developing meaning.

Total yes responses: ____

Total no responses: ____

Surprising yes and no responses:

_____

_____

_____

Emotional reaction to these responses:

_____

_____

_____

Thoughts that emerge as you reflect back:

_____

_____

_____

After completing the quiz and taking time to reflect, I think it is time to transition into exploring the skill set that encompasses MEANING. Table 4.1 is a quick and easy guide to assist you as you proceed through this chapter. Pause and think or take a break when you need to.

TEXTBOX 4.1. MEANING

M: Master the art of self-love
E: Express emotions in a healthy way
A: Assertive with wants and needs
N: New identity

I: Intentional living

N: New you, New life

G: Grieve the relationship

M: Mastering the Art of Self-Love

Let's begin with considering the importance of *mastering* the art of self-love. Typically, there exist various perspectives on self-love. There are those who feel self-love is overrated, that we are raising children who cannot handle hard things in their lives and get their feelings hurt easily. The idea emphasizes that these children will grow up unable to manage stressors in life. Some have been taught that loving others is more important than loving oneself. There is an emphasis on servanthood, putting others' needs ahead of self, and being selfless. Striking a healthy balance between the two, balancing loving ourselves and loving others, is essential. And this is very unlike the characteristics of a person with NPD. Remember, narcissists only think of themselves and their needs, and they verbally express things to stroke their high ego at the expense of others. Why am I mentioning this? Many survivors of NPD abuse have often been told by the abuser that the *victim* is the narcissist. This is quite confusing, especially as it potentially coincides with the victim being told over and again that they are selfish. It makes them question where their allegiance should lie and if they are truly self-centered. The fact that they question if they are self-centered is a good sign of their capacity for self-reflection and awareness. Although some folks raised by a narcissist develop the disorder, you, reader, are likely not one.

To begin the process of loving yourself, first, give yourself permission to focus on just yourself for a moment—or at least for the length of this book. Next, is beginning to practice some self-compassion. What is self-compassion? From my experience, I can say this means giving yourself permission to be human, flawed, emotional, analytical, special, and educated, as well as to be treated with respect in the same way you'd treat another human being. I can almost guarantee that you give your NPD abuser and others lots of patience and self-compassion. It is time to do the same for yourself. The subsequent step is reflecting upon your own environment regarding love.

Our childhood environment influences how we understand the concept of love. We are taught love and empathy from our parents/caregivers, but they can also teach us that love is conditional and dependent upon a multitude of factors. If your parent was the narcissist, they might have engaged in a variation of love bombing, possibly saying things such as "I love you more than anyone ever will" or "You don't love me if you do not do this for me or if you do not listen." There can be quite a variation. Consider a young child who is trying to navigate that concept of love. Before we can understand that word, it is necessary to understand that it is linked to attachment, as I discussed in an earlier chapter. If we get our needs met (e.g., the need for food, shelter, and attention), we can experience a sense of calm and peace, which can later resonate in our minds as love.

Developmental theorists have differing beliefs concerning how individuals learn about love and how it resonates within their lives as they grow from children to adults, but a common factor they share upholds the influence of primary caregivers on a child's future interactions with others and their understanding of self in relation to others (Beckett & Taylor, 2019). As a child ages and grows into an adult, the interactions between that individual and other adults influence their perceptions of self-love and their love for others. This is particularly true when the adult child witnesses how other families, relationships, and peers engage with one another. I remember watching other families and noticing how they exhibited love for one another without arguing or belittling. I then began to realize that there were other ways for individuals to experience and express love, and it provided both a sense of awareness and confusion. It is quite common to ask yourself, Why don't I experience love in the same manner as others? There is hope! Receiving love from another (e.g., teacher, professor, caregiver, friend, or partner) can help us to see how love is—or how it could be. If you have heard the words "I love you," yet there is no connection, no emotional feeling or behavior of love attached to the words, it can be confusing. Without having the connected experience of love, you might enter a relationship with a partner or friendship that is also unloving. And it is no wonder! We seek out similar characteristics in relationships, whether we are cognizant of that or not. It is easier to relate to someone who's had a similar experience, as it is more challenging to learn and engage with a new pattern. So if you've never had a reason to love yourself and have preferred to focus on others, you may find that pattern continuing in future relationships. It can feel good to help other people at the initial stages of the relationship, but it then can be deflating once you realize that you are doing all the work in offering love. It is normal to you, and thus, you do not expect anything different. I am saying that you deserve more! Narcissistic relationships are all about them—not you. It is now time to focus on yourself.

Finally, consider the concept of love you have as an adult. Is it oriented toward action or a feeling? It is hard to differentiate between love as an action or a feeling, so what do we do? Learn to love yourself. There is truth to the adage "You have to learn to love yourself before you can love someone else." We have heard this over and again in our lives. If we do not love ourselves, it is quite hard to love someone else. Over time, we learn a lot from our interactions with others, and I have found whether the reflection is healthy or unhealthy, the individuals we engage mirror who we are. After being in a meditation one evening, this phrase came to me: "Each soul comes into our lives, bearing a gift, a mirror reflection of ourselves, and has a lesson to teach us." I rediscover the truth in these words as I interact with individuals in my life. As I watch others, I learn something about myself, including how much I self-deprecate and how unsure I am of how to connect with others and to value myself. Ask yourself, What does self-love look like? It first includes asking for help, which you have done by picking up this book. Then take the time to validate who you are as a person. As a human being, you have the right to be here on this earth. You have a purpose, talents, gifts, strengths, and limitations. Stop for a minute and reflect upon who you are, and ask yourself if you live according to your values or if you are living according to someone else's values. You have a right to be you and to live according to your values. Values relate to work, social connections, intimate connections, spirituality, and philanthropy.

William Glasser, in his work on choice/reality therapy, would ask clients how they get their need for love met in their life. We explore his theory more in Chapter 12. A common answer given is through a higher power, parents, or a partner. What about self-love for those who are not able to get this need met by others? It is important to step back and be proud of who you are. I encourage you to take at least 3 minutes each day, typically at the end of the day, to reflect upon your accomplishments. It might be as simple as noting that you are living with integrity when others around you are not or that you are showing up as an advocate for someone when others do not. Take some moments. Tell yourself, "You are worthy of love." The more you and I say it, the more we will believe it, for our thoughts are very powerful.

E: Express Emotions in a Healthy Way

Now let's delve into the second letter, E, in the acronym of MEANING by evaluating the importance of expressing emotions in a healthy way. I know from my own personal story how I learned to mute my emotions. Experiencing my emotions did not do anything for me. In fact, they caused me more problems because I was told that I was causing others' emotional pain. This chastisement reinforced my belief that if I was the cause of emotional pain, then I needed to control my emotions. The problem with controlling emotions is that the more you try to control them—the more you push down, hold off, and overcontrol—the faster you'll reach the point where your emotions explode or completely shut down, leaving you with no opinion or emotional response. Neither is healthy or preferred. Emotions do not have to be good or bad; they just are. We have emotions for a reason: they help us to navigate our lives when we have good or bad news or experiences. However, we do need to make sure that we are familiar with the emotions that all humans have.

I explore emotional regulation in more detail in Chapter 9, but as we explore it here, I ask you to consider the range of emotions you've had throughout your life. Ask yourself, What is the strongest emotion I experience? Is it happiness, worry, frustration, anger, or another emotion? It is useful to spend time evaluating your emotions so that you are aware of the range of emotions you can feel; this also helps you validate an emotion and then let it pass. In narcissistic relationships we may have been taught that our emotions are not okay and the emotions of others are more important. I still battle with that in my own life, and you may too. How do we validate our emotions? We need to acknowledge that what we are feeling is valid when our emotions emerge. If it is a long-standing, unhealthy emotion, such as depression, you need to work on it. However, if you're feeling sadness (vs. depression), anger (vs. rage), nervousness (vs. anxiety), that is okay. You have the right to be sad, angry, or nervous. Part of our expressing emotions in a healthy way is acknowledging what we are feeling, stopping for a minute to reflect, and then deciding our next steps regarding behavior. Instead of yelling at someone, consider effective ways to communicate. If you are sad, it is okay to cry. If you are frustrated, vent with a friend. If you are angry, be assertive (vs. aggressive).

A: Assertive With Needs and Wants

As we delve into the third letter, A, of the acronym MEANING, we explore how to be assertive with our wants and needs. We have already acknowledged that expressing individual wants and needs while in an NPD relationship is frowned upon, as the primary focuses for a narcissist are their own wants and needs. As we take steps in exploring assertiveness, we tackle why you need to learn it (and delve deeper into it through discussing interpersonal effectiveness in Chapter 8) .

If you grew up in an environment or are currently in an environment with someone with NPD, you know all too well that the only voice that matters in the relationship is that of the narcissist. On the one hand, this voice can be harsh and then, on the other hand, kind. Let me explain. They might make statements about your looks, skills, parenting, work, opinions, and being that break you down instead of lift you up. If you inquire about it further and ask to hear about your strengths, not your weaknesses, you likely will be told you are "being too sensitive" or "can't take the truth," and thus, you shut down and go into your shell. Oftentimes, they excuse their comments, saying that they tell the truth, are just blunt, or have greater knowledge than you (or others). The reality is they use manipulation and aggressiveness, not assertiveness, to bully someone into agreeing with them. They want you to submit and follow without question. If we hear enough bad things about ourselves, we believe them and often go out of our way to try and find ways to fix them. Unfortunately, even if you were to earn your PhD and the NPD person were to only have a high school diploma, they would still find a way to break you down. They may even say, "You think you are smarter than everyone else, but you're not smarter than me just because you went to college." It is a win-lose situation, with a win for the narcissist and a loss for the you.

I hope you can see why it is important to learn and practice assertiveness, and I am sure you are wondering, How did I not notice this was happening? Well, consider who you were before you connected with this individual with NPD—specifically, consider your communication style. Were you already a person who tended to please others and not say no? Were you always amenable? If so, it is likely you were more passive and accepting of someone else taking the lead. This is fertile ground for a narcissist because they perceive that an individual who is passive is easily manipulated and controlled. It happens slowly until the narcissist has built trust and a connection with you, and it will take some time to see the reality underneath. The problem with being passive—believe me, I was for many years and still battle it—is the passive individual lacks their voice for fear of hurting others, which keeps them in internal turmoil while outwardly compliant. That is why you may find yourself connected to a narcissist and not even know it for months or years. Narcissists, tend to be quite passive-aggressive, then aggressive, but they are neither passive nor assertive. They may claim they are being assertive, but they are being aggressive. Let's cover some brief definitions of the differences in these styles of communication.

As noted earlier, a passive communicator tends to be a people pleaser, does not say no to requests even when they do not want to do them, has poor boundaries, and is often publicly labeled as a doormat. Someone who is passive-aggressive is considered to be inconsistent, that they talk out of both sides of their mouths. It is common for some of us readers to fall into this category, especially as we are working on being less passive and more assertive. We can move along the continuum as a passive individual in seeking to say no, set boundaries, and speak up, but we face the tendency to say one thing and do another. For example, you may not want to help a friend move their items to a new house. Someone with a passive-aggressive style might say, "Sure I will be there," but then they mysteriously become ill and don't show up. In reality, they just did not want to say no when asked. People exhibiting these behaviors can be publicly viewed as saboteurs. Aggressive is someone who doesn't care about others' boundaries, gets in folks' faces, tramples all over others' feelings and emotions with a desire to win, and has the capacity to be verbally, emotionally, or physically violent. These folks don't take no for an answer, so you can see how someone who is either passive or passive-aggressive can be easily overtaken by someone who is aggressive. Please have hope, as we all can learn to be assertive. Assertive people listen within themselves to what they want to do, and they set boundaries, express emotions and needs, and value the needs of others. Assertive individuals have mastered the art of using "I" statements, living according to their principles and values, upholding their boundaries, and being honest. In Chapter 8 we delve into the specific interpersonal effectiveness skills that go along with assertiveness.

N: New Identity

Continuing with the acronym of MEANING, let's delve a bit into the fourth letter, N, and what it means to have a new identity. As you continue to read through this chapter, remember that you are growing. Any exposure we have to new information helps us grow, which sparks change and evokes the idea of something new. When we are taking on a new role, there is no way others will not see the shift. I have heard clients over the years talk about the change they've seen in others or the people in their lives seeing the clients' changes. Developing and having a new identity can be quite scary because it means we might lose folks in our lives who are accustomed to our old selves. As I reflect upon my own life, I am aware that I've had many folks come in and out of my life, particularly during times of change, which I know was spurred by their dislike for me no longer being a doormat or easily following their desires. I could feel the disconnect due to the lack of reciprocity in the relationship, whether that was between friends, family, or coworkers, and my new identity and growth prompted me to no longer need this connection. I am sure you've uttered, "I will change," but then when you actually do, folks try to draw you back into the old way of being. It is common to vacillate back and forth between identities until you reach a personal realization that going back to your old ways is almost like dying to self. Conforming to an old way of self can be not only emotionally but physically stressful.

Stop for a minute, and consider your own life history. Think about who you were before your connection to the individual with NPD. I encourage you to write down that reflection on page 67. Next, consider your identity after this connection with the NPD abuser. Is it the same or different? Why?

Take time to reflect and write down your responses. Finally, you will need to do some future-oriented considerations: What would your new identity look like and how will you behave after disconnecting from the individual with NPD? Write this reflection down as well.

Before:

_____

_____

_____

During:

_____

_____

_____

After:

_____

_____

_____

After writing down your responses, take a deep belly breath. Remember, you have the right to change your mind at any moment and to live according to your values and the new you. If a relationship is hurtful, nonreciprocal, controlling, and shaming, it's time for you to work toward your new identity. Chapter 5 delves into how you can work toward expressing that authentic self.

I: Intentional Living

Now that you are aware of the importance of a new identity, with change comes the need to live intentionally, which is the fifth area of focus in the MEANING acronym. Let's first break down the words so we have a context regarding why we should live intentionally. The word *intention* focuses on an aim, or plan. When we think about planning, we must consider the importance of acting or doing. So, to be intentional, we must understand the action of a plan. Part of making a plan involves understanding the cognitive and behavioral process. We think about what we want to do, write it down, and then take steps to make it happen. Writing down the plan makes us more likely to take action. As you can see, the intention is multifaceted—and exciting!

When we examining the word *living*, we may first think that if we are not dead, then we are living. I think it's necessary to add some perspective to this. I love the line in *Shawshank Redemption* when Morgan Freeman's character Red says, "Get busy living or get busy dying" (Darabont, 1994, 1:25). We have a choice in all that we do, so while we are living, we must ask ourselves, What does living look like for me? How does this compare to how I want to live? Everyone's definition is very different. If you feel as though life is passing you by and you are not really being your authentic self, adhering to your own needs and wants, then it is time to adapt. The reality is that the more you live your new identity, the more you will begin to live intentionally. How? You will no longer want to be in the same position you've been in, and you might even need to plan your escape from that situation. Thus, you will need to set a plan or aim to make these changes an active part of your life by setting your intention. This is explored further in Chapter 5, which delves into the very vulnerable act of risk taking.

N: New You, New Life

As you are working toward making MEANING out of your experience, you have been prompted to consider your new identity and living intentionally; with these accomplished, you can begin to be the new you within a new life. Working with survivors of narcissistic abuse, I've found it is quite common for this to be a slow process. There is no quick turnaround where we learn the information, see meaning in our experience, and then change within a week. Change takes time. In fact, the theoretical model of change reiterates that it takes quite some time to move from a lack of awareness to awareness and then action.

In the late 1970s, Prochaska and Diclemente (1983) developed the idea that when individuals need or want a change, they must go through certain cognitive stages. These stages are not linear, and in fact, individuals vacillate between the stages. They coined this process the transtheoretical model, or stages of change (Prochaska & DiClemente, 1983). When I work with clients and see that they have created a plan with an aim to take action and yet seem stuck, I evaluate where they are in the stages of change. So let's explore a bit further.

Prochaska and DiClemente (1983) noted that individuals move through six stages of change, which include precontemplation, contemplation, preparation, action, maintenance, and termination. Let's think of this regarding the relationship with an NPD abuser. In the precontemplation stage, people do not intend to take any action, because there is lack of awareness of the problem. This might be you. Someone may have purchased this book for you and asked you to read it, or maybe you bought it because you were intrigued by the title, thinking you might be connected to an NPD abuser. It is normal to not be sure if this applies to you. The next stage is contemplation, where you recognize that there is a problem but are not quite sure how to proceed as you weigh the pros and cons. If this is you, then you picked up this book with the awareness of a problem. But you might be asking yourself, How can this book help me? You might have reviewed other books and considered other options as well. Regardless, I am glad you have this book in front of you.

Next is preparation, which occurs when you are not in denial that there is a problem, you have already explored the pros and cons, and now you are ready for a change and are preparing for it. This might be what led you to this book, to review some videos, to talk with friends, to self-reflecting, and so forth. At this stage you want to be in a stage of preparation, and as was mentioned earlier in this chapter, you want to be intentional and smart about it because you are aware this is healthier. This is the sweet spot to be in, and it may be that you are at this stage for a while—that is normal. I was at this stage for quite some time before I took the leap to action. This was when I did a lot of soul searching, journaling, and reflecting so that my behavior could shift.

Then, there is readiness for the action phase of change. You have begun to make some changes, and you intend to move forward into more change. Thus, reading this book might be one more step on your path to maintaining the change. I often say that to maintain the change it takes continued self-work, boundaries maintenance (as we talked about under assertiveness), and consideration of all the avenues needed to maintain the new behaviors. The maintenance phase is achieved when someone has maintained the behavior for a while and has not relapsed. It can be easy to relapse in a narcissistic relationship, so do not beat yourself up about it. When we get enough distance to maintain our behavioral change, sometimes the flying monkeys (people the NPD abuser sends out to spy on us) may enter your life and try to draw you back to the narcissist and old behaviors. The final stage is termination, which happens when you no longer engage in behaviors that don't serve you, so the new you and new life can take hold. Realistically, as NPD survivors, we can live our new life, and there will be folks who still try and draw us back to the NPD abuser. Remember that each day is a new one. You can always start over. Additional elements of making choices using theoretical steps are explored in Chapter 12.

G: Grieve the Relationship

Part of being new is realizing that, to draw MEANING in our lives, we must grieve the relationship. This grieving of the relationship involves several things. We often associate grief with the death of someone close to us. However, we can grieve what we did not receive from the relationship: empathy, love, support, compassion, or validation. We also need to grieve the bond we had with that individual. As I noted in Chapter 3 regarding attachment, we can develop unhealthy attachment patterns to individuals, and with that, it can be challenging to disconnect from that person or situation because it may be all that we know. We can get into the cycle of thinking, "I should or could give this person another chance," "I just need to understand their situation better," or "I should not expect so much from others." I thought this—and so much more—for years, but when I finally stepped back and realized that my NPD abuser would not change, I could grieve what I never got from the relationship. Remember that you can grieve this relationship whether you stay connected with this person or not. As you begin to change, the relationship will look different, and there will be some pain that grieves you. We explore this further in Chapter 11.

I know that exploring MEANING is quite heavy, as there are many small steps we need to take to build up to finding meaning in the relationship; we do this so that we can begin to EVOLVE. Our growth leads to a natural unfolding of this evolution. If you take nothing else away from this chapter, I hope that you can walk away with the understanding that we learn a lot from our experiences. Since you have this book in your hand, you have exhibited interest in looking at a new way of being in your life, one that is healthy and peaceful. Let's do a bit more reflection before closing out this chapter.

Reflective Journaling

Which section of the MEANING acronym stands out to you? Why?

_____

_____

_____

What part of the MEANING acronym do you need to work on the most? How do you intend to do this?

_____

_____

_____

CHAPTER 5

~

Helping Survivors to EVOLVE

I am glad that you have stuck with me through this process of understanding exposure to NPD abuse. In the last chapter, you had the opportunity to complete a quiz to gain self-knowledge about your exposure to NPD abuse. The outlined characteristics provide perspective regarding how their traits influence your daily living. After the assessment you bravely walked through the elements of recognizing the MEANING that can be drawn from your experience to NPD exposure. Now it is time to think about how you or other survivors of NPD abuse can begin to EVOLVE.

Before I break down this acronym further, I would like for you to consider what it means to evolve. For me, evolution brings to mind a gradual change occurring over time that requires small steps, whether they be conscious or not. This means that sometimes, you have awareness of change unfolding, while, at other times, you have no awareness. Evolving takes time. Let's examine what we explore in this chapter: You will learn the importance of E, exploring your NPD abuse story; V, the importance of self-validation of these experiences; O, being open to new ideas, experiences, and people; L, learning that life can and will be different when the decision is made for change; V, taking a risk with being vulnerable to a new life; and E, beginning to express the new developing self. It is useful to see this broken down in a visual way (see Textbox 5.1) so you can refer to it as we delve deeper into each of the components.

TEXTBOX 5.1. EVOLVE

E: Exploring your NPD abuse story
V: Validating these experiences

O: Open expression to new ideas, experiences, and people
L: Learning that life can be different and change is possible
V: Vulnerability with self
E: Expressing the developing self

E: Exploring Your NPD Abuse Story

Part of evolving includes gaining an awareness of our story—the story that contributes to who we are, and sharing that story is very powerful. Whether you are the survivor or are seeking to help a survivor, the E letter of the acronym reminds us to stop and explore NPD exposure and experiences.

Storytelling has been passed down across communities, cultures, and families (Bruner, 2002). I often brag that my husband is the best storyteller, and when my children were young, there were many nights that they would say, "Daddy, tell me a story." I was not the storyteller, and they preferred his unique and creative tales to my (less exciting) ones. I always told him to write them down because they were so good. There are imaginative stories, like his, but there are also true stories that tell of our lives. They get passed down from generation to generation, while at other times, stories are not shared because they are too painful. I've often heard clients say they would prefer not to remember. However, to begin evolving, you must be willing to share even the most painful stories of your life, including your exposure to NPD, with a safe individual. Landrum et al. (2019) explained that storytelling is a teaching tool that highlights how to not repeat a pattern. Consider the history of wars, genocides, and other atrocities in our world. I know when I studied history, we were told we must know history so we do not repeat it. It is the same here: it benefits you to know that exploring your story helps remind you of what happened; get support for what happened; seek to evaluate how it contributes to your thoughts, beliefs, emotions, and functioning; and be aware so you can watch out for red flags in the future. Most of you are likely very afraid that you may fall prey to an NPD abuser's level of manipulation again, that you may fall for a romantic partner or be exposed to someone else who is a NPD abuser. Of course, we always run that risk in our lives. We cannot mind read, predict, or know everything about another person, but I can tell you from my own work of sharing my story that I am much more aware of the signs of narcissistic behaviors than I was before I shared my story.

With exploring your story, consider what you would like to share. Your story is connected to a multitude of experiences, not just one, but we need to start somewhere. Your exposure to NPD abuse may be current, or it may be historical, having begun in your childhood. As a result, each person's story will be unique. I encourage you to begin with the first memory in your life when you were aware that something was different about this relationship. You may not be sure what was different about it, but you knew that it was, which caused you to stop and reflect.

Here is a way to break down the story into a few stages: First, take a minute to stop and reflect. Examine the quiz you took in the last chapter, and reflect on the times you noticed you felt guilty for something you did not do, responsible for your NPD abuser's emotions, or like you were the primary problem in the relationship. Second, take a moment to reflect, then write down the story that is emerging. Of course, we all have variations of our story, but do not edit it or sensor yourself. Just write it. This form of automatic writing doesn't filter the content, whether we are writing in a journal or typing. Then take a moment to read back over that story, and ask yourself a few questions regarding what unfolded in the writing.

Here is space to reflect on one of the stories from your NPD exposure. Additional space is available in the back of the book.

What role did I play in this story?

What role did the NPD abuser play in this story?

What was the outcome of this story?

What emotions remain(ed) after it all unfolded?

What you will notice is that this is only one of several stories you could share. You have likely gained a new perspective regarding the physical, emotional, and overall behavioral impact the NPD abuser had on you. There is only room in this part of the chapter to share one story, but I know from my own experience that there are multiple. You might be asking, Why should I reflect on and write a story? Well, your story is powerful and worthy of being shared, and we remember the stories that evoked our emotions. When your story occurred, you may have not felt empowered or supported to act, but now you can. You have the right to change the ending of your story. Your experience is relevant and can help to influence and validate your experience.

V: Validating These Experiences

Now that you have shared this story, you do not have to share it again, but you may find sharing with someone safe is beneficial; this could be a close friend or even a professional helper. This leads us to the next letter of EVOLVE, V for validation. All human beings want to be validated, but there are so many folks who never feel that they have been heard or understood, much less validated, regarding their experience. Validation does not mean the listener condones the situation or judges the story; rather, they respond with empathy, and you feel your experience was understood and accepted, as well as that you have a right to the thoughts, emotions, and behaviors you exhibited at the time. You are likely thinking that no one will ever validate your experience, because so many folks in your life have been brainwashed or manipulated by the NPD abuser. You may be correct, but an alternative option is self-validation. I learned a long time ago that if I wait for other individuals to validate my experiences, I will never get any validation. I've waited and waited with no outcome except for advice given on how to manage my relationship with the NPD abuser. Realistically, I'd already thought of every piece of advice I'd received, and it was therefore not helpful to be told what to do. So I had to learn to self-validate my experience. What does it mean to self-validate?

There are many different perceptions regarding self-validation. Since we explored what validation from others looks like, let's consider how we can provide empathy and understanding to ourselves. It can be easier to be very understanding of others, including your NPD abuser, and to put your own validation on the back burner. In fact, in an NPD relationship, you were not allowed to be the center of attention, and your identity and needs were put on the back burner. Waiting for validation from the narcissist or even from others is often fruitless. So consider some ways you can validate yourself and your experiences. First, even if you want to nitpick the story(ies) that you shared, stop yourself. Tell yourself that your experience, whether believed or not, is, according to your memory, what you actually went through, and it's had a lasting impact. Next, remind yourself that you have the right to the thoughts and emotions that emerged when you wrote this story and that will emerge in the future upon further reflection. Then draw from the story, and ask yourself, What strengths did I draw from to manage that situation at that time? What has this taught me? Next, challenge your thoughts and remind yourself that you did the best that you could at the time, take responsibility for how you responded, and then tell yourself, "I can move on from it now. I no longer have to beat myself up if for not taking action or responding like I would now." Finally, remind yourself that you are taking charge of your life and are making radical changes. Guess what? You just self-validated.

O: Open Expression to New Ideas, Experiences, and People

Now that you are no longer waiting for someone else to validate you, there is a tool in your toolbox you can use to assist yourself in those difficult moments when others are not able to understand you. As we continue with the acronym EVOLVE, we now examine O, which stands for open expression to new ideas, experiences, and people. Openness is very hard, especially when we have been hurt by others we thought were genuine, kind, and had our best interests at heart. We are blindsided when we realize that the person we thought we could trust was actually the very person who sabotaged and likely seemed to ruin our lives. Evolving includes the process of examining that you are in a process of change.

In the counseling field, there is a theory called the transtheoretical model of change, often referred to as change theory. When I was first exposed to change theory, it slipped into my awareness and then quickly out again. It didn't stick until I started working with folks who were struggling with behavioral change: wanting to eat better, exercise more, stop a bad habit, get out of a relationship, and so forth. As I worked on my own healing and on the healing of others exposed to NPD abuse, I found the theory of change becoming relevant. According to change theory, being open to new people and experiences does not necessarily mean that you are taking steps (that comes later in the stages). Thus, it is important to assess both where you are in the stages of change and how to begin the process of being open to the new you. We know that in precontemplation, you are unaware that a change is needed. This is likely where you found yourself at the beginning of your NPD relationship. Someone on the outside could potentially see that change is needed, but you personally cannot. As noted in the last chapter, contemplation occurs when you are intending to begin a new and healthier behavior in the future because you finally recognize there is a problem. Realistically, this may be where you are right now, and that suggests that you are *open*, which is okay because this is difficult: you might be going back and forth between wanting to change and not. We can enter and exit these stages; it can take some time to move from precontemplation to contemplation to action, but right now, in this moment, to be open is to be contemplating that something needs to change. Take some time to assess where you are, and realize that you are right where you need to be right now. This sets you up for the next level of evolving.

L: Learning That Life Can Be Different and Change Is Possible

By knowing where you are in the stage of change, you can see the power of learning. The next level of EVOLVING is learning (L) that life can be different, that change is possible, and this has already begun for you. You already established that you are open to learning by picking up this book, and you've likely been reinforcing this as you explored where you are in the stages of change. Thus, you are learning from not only this book but from the varied ways you have self-reflected and grown in your self-awareness. As a counselor-educator, I know that learning is a lifelong process, and I value learning in all aspects of life. We learn from not only formal but informal education, which include life experiences.

Recently, there has been a shift for many individuals leaving high school, many of whom are not pursuing higher education. Many companies are going back to the apprentice-style method of learning, which is passed on by a senior member in the profession. In some ways, this is similar to the setup in formal education, where students learn from professors who are considered senior members or mentors in their fields. So it is not a far stretch to consider that there are numerous decisions individuals can make regarding their learning. When it comes to exposure to NPD abuse, for change to happen, it is important that we confront what we've experienced, reflect on it, learn from it, and then move forward toward new decisions based on what we've learned. As is commonly said, "We are either growing or we are dying." Think about the flowers: they grow and bloom, and then they die. Like all of nature, to which we are connected, we are born and then we die—but there is a broad gap with lots of growth in-between. This is connected to self-education and learning so patterns do not repeat. It is important to know that you can change, and with change comes power. But to be open to change, we must be vulnerable.

V: Vulnerability With Self

Vulnerability is very scary, but it is essential to being our authentic self. The next letter of EVOLVING is V for vulnerability. I remember years ago, I was exploring myself from varying angles, including my childlike side, my wounded child, and then my adult perspective. We often want to abandon the characteristics of a child and be an adult, with all the responsibilities. Remember: responsibilities are necessary, but the child within is still there, crying to get out. Sometimes, that inner child is who we really are. I remember when I was very young, I was outspoken, brave, loud, and unashamed—a free spirit. As time unfolded and life experiences happened, I emotionally aged and felt like an adult at the age of 12. Now that I am older, I have been again desiring to be that free-spirited child, my true self, who was stomped down by protective parts of me. Many individuals have read the work of Brené Brown and her research on vulnerability. She truly embodies the meaning of vulnerability. I have found that one way to get to our authentic self is through self-evaluation and to metaphorically emotionally strip ourselves of all titles. We all play roles, and as adults, we spend most of our lives either as caregivers or workers. When we strip away the title of mom, dad, employee, employer, caregiver, friend, parent, grandmother, and on and on, all we are left with is our figurative naked selves; hence why it can be so difficult for individuals to retire. They filled their lives and based their identities on the work they did every day. Being vulnerable requires that we strip away our facades, our titles, our egos, and even disconnect to those things that are inauthentic to be vulnerable to new experiences and people.

To be vulnerable requires some work. I encourage you to take a few minutes and assess some things. First, what were you taught about being vulnerable when you were growing up? Some of us were told that we should never have our guard down or we could be hurt. Or we may have had very loose boundaries, gotten hurt, and come to consider vulnerability as risky. Second, ask yourself, When have I been vulnerable and what were the outcomes in my life? I have been vulnerable, and it backfired on me, while other times, the risk paid off. These two questions encourage awareness of self and help you to understand and accept yourself as you are. After reflecting upon these questions, consider what is honest and true about you. What part of yourself have you been afraid to show others due to fear of their judgment? Maybe you like something that is against the norm of your community, peer group, or family, so you spend your life pretending to be something or someone you are not. I know in my younger years, I spent so much time just wanting to be liked, even loved. This went back to my attachment style, as explored in an earlier chapter. I sought out acceptance and connection, but it would often fall short. Now that I look back on my life, I realize this lack of connection occurred because I was not vulnerable in who I was. Ask yourself this next question: Is it worth it to be vulnerable so others can see my authentic self?

Once you have reflected on the true you, your next step is to accept all your parts and to break free from seeking approval in your vulnerable moments. This is easier said than done, isn't it? Remember what we explored about change earlier in this chapter: it is a process, and not a quick one. It reminds me of the Queen song, "I Want to Break Free." We need to release our pretenses and be ourselves at some point. Feel free to use the lines below to reflect on these questions.

What were you taught about being vulnerable when you were growing up?

_____

_____

_____

Consider when you have been vulnerable. What was the outcome of that in your life?

_____

_____

_____

What part of yourself have you been afraid to show others due to fear of their judgment?

_____

_____

_____

What one behavioral step will you take to show up vulnerably as your authentic self?

_____

_____

_____

E: Expressing the Developing Self

Now that we have tackled the first five letters of EVOLVE, it is important to focus on the final letter, E, which stands for the expression of a new, developing self. There are a variety of action elements in EVOLVE, and the final need—expressing the new self—is now ready to develop. Your self is not fully solidified; it is clearly adapting and changing regardless of whether we want it to or not. As I noted earlier, we are always changing. When you consider the expression of self, remember that it is developing. Just like with human physical growth and development, we are always mentally and emotionally growing and developing.

Learning theory, a developmental theory, reiterates what we talked about earlier in this chapter regarding learning that life can be different. As a clay potter, I resonate with using the metaphor of shaping and molding clay to describe how children are formed during development. Of course, with clay, it can turn out beautifully—or it can be destroyed. Watson (1924), when exploring development, noted that children are lumps of clay that are shaped and molded by their environment. This makes sense when we explore vulnerability with our authentic self: if we are in the hands of a potter (our caregivers), we are not quite sure how we will turn out. However, we do know that before we go into their hands, we are genetically one way and their environmental influences may shape us in a different way. Expression of self involves taking a risk with who you are, even after you've been shaped and formed. When I finish molding clay, then bisque fire it, glaze it, and put it on display, everyone perceives that piece differently, defining it in different ways. Well, you are the creator of your piece, yourself. Now it is time to express yourself. Consider how you can express your authentic self in a small way.

What are your interests?

_____

_____

_____

What are your hobbies?

_____

_____

_____

How do you express yourself?

_____

_____

_____

How do you relax when you are stressed?

_____

_____

_____

We have delved into all the elements of EVOLVE, which emphasize the importance of sharing your story of NPD abuse and then providing a way to self-validate your experiences. We all need to feel as though what we say is important, understood, and believed. Once your story is shared, you may feel a sense of relief, like a weight is lifted off your shoulders, and you can step back and say, "I am making it. I can begin to be open to new people, ideas and experiences." Part of this process involves learning from our past and then continuing to learn as we move through life. If we are to grow and learn, we need to be vulnerable in ways that highlight our true selves instead of laying ourselves out to be hurt again. It is quite vulnerable to authentically be who we are. Finally, the more we know, the more we are open and the more we are willing to express ourselves across all domains of life, including in our communities, in our families, and at work.

Let's do a bit more reflection before closing out this chapter.

Reflective Journaling

What emotions emerge as you think about evolving and changing?

_____

_____

Part of evolving is learning new ways of being. This includes shifting from an old to a new self. How can you encourage this process in your own life?

_____

_____

_____

CHAPTER 6

~

Survive and VENTURE
Into a New Life

I hope you can begin to be empowered to share your story without fear and be open to what may unfold as you gain your voice within the NPD abusive relationship. As we continue on this journey, remember what you have accomplished so far. You are not only aware of the characteristics of NPD, but you are able to evaluate the impact of this relationship. Once you are aware of the impact, you can begin the process of moving beyond understanding narcissism and its impact on you to begin the process of personal healing. You have tackled the difficulty of finding MEANING from these experiences, begun the process of EVOLVING, and now you are ready to call yourself a survivor and begin your VENTURE into a new life. Venturing out into the unfamiliar is risky. The risk can evoke your fear, especially after being in a relationship where the NPD abuser dictated your every step and decision. This chapter provides some context to help you take steps toward being a new you. Please review Table 6.1 to explore the acronym VENTURE further. You will learn the importance of V, valuing and not minimizing your experiences, which then leads into E, exploring the story of other aspects of your life because you are far more than an NPD abuse survivor, and you have other things in your life that define you. After you have explored yourself further, you can begin to N, navigate the elements of a new identity and then consider plans to accomplish it. As you navigate through this book, it is important to take T, time out to reflect on where you have come from and where you are going. It can be overwhelming, but hang in there, it is possible. Sometimes, this time out can be a catalyst to helping you U, understand the past to learn to navigate a new future, which promotes openness to R, reinventing yourself with new skills, and working toward E, experiencing a new life.

TEXTBOX 6.1. VENTURE

V: Valuing your experiences
E: Exploring other aspects of your life story
N: Navigating the elements of a new identity
T: Time out to reflect
U: Understanding the past and the lessons learned to navigate a new future
R: Reinventing yourself
E: Experiencing a new life

Before delving into each of the components one by one, pause. Consider your thoughts about the two words in the title of this chapter: survive and venture. Survival is a strong word. I have considered myself a survivor in two contexts: NPD abuse and breast cancer. Think about areas in your life where you consider yourself a survivor. I prefer the word survivor versus victim because it reminds me that I persevered through challenges, overcoming something others may not have survived, and I am still standing. Survival also conjures up considerations of resilience. I would hear individuals say that I was strong, a survivor, and resilient. While pursuing my doctoral degree, I was interested in exploring what makes an individual resilient. Resilient individuals can bounce back medically and mentally after difficult situations. But what makes some folks more resilient than others? Individuals develop resilience after exposure to some form of adversity and have the ability to positively adapt or bounce back after the adversity. Contributing factors to resilience have both genetic and environmental influences that begin in infancy and continue into adulthood (Vella & Pai, 2019). I urge you to see yourself as a resilient survivor. For a clearer picture, consider self-reflection. I would like you to stop and take 5 minutes to answer the following questions about aspects of your life that might contribute to your resilience. As you write your answers down, consider which ones you think of fondly and which are more challenging. Maybe there are some you have a difficult time adequately processing, as your mind shielded you from the pain of those experiences. You can write your responses as a time line, in bullet points, or in a few sentences.

Explore up to six experiences you've had in your life.

_____

_____

_____

_____

_____

_____

_____

_____

_____

_____

What events, people, or situations have influenced you?

_____

_____

_____

_____

_____

_____

_____

_____

_____

After reflecting on these experiences, do you find you can categorize yourself as a resilient survivor? I encourage you to examine your survival *despite* the obstacles you have encountered. Remember, resilient people, like yourself, have survived, and they often seek answers in their desire to change. Taking the time to reflect sets you up to consider, process, and plan for an adventure. You may not be convinced yet, but hopefully, you will feel more confident as we continue moving through this chapter.

The term *adventure*, a noun, is considered a root word for venture. Venture, as an element of adventure, is a verb that alludes to action. Consider that when you are venturing, you are doing/going/making something. When I think of venturing, I think of hiking in the mountains, riding a motorcycle down a country road on a beautiful day, taking a long trip, or starting something new. Adventures are often planned out, but we cannot predict every twist and turn, because life throws us unpredictable situations. From my past and present experiences (and, I predict, my future ones as well), I am aware that adventures can have varied outcomes. They can be good or bad, pleasant or unpleasant, risky or safe, difficult or easy, but they share a common element: when we venture, we make a choice to go on the journey. Sometimes, we have folks who will come along with us, while, at other times, it is a solo trip. Planning is a part of this process, along with navigating how we are to achieve it. This applies both when we're traveling and when we're venturing into new territory. You may potentially venture into this new territory without your NPD abuser, or if you are still connected with them, you might find yourself empowered to begin venturing into new and uncharted territory.

V: Valuing Your Experiences

Now that we have explored survival, resilience, and adventure, it is time to explore the elements of VENTURE a bit closer. Let's begin by exploring V, which stands for valuing your experiences. After living with or being around narcissists, you know that your perspective, accomplishments, heartaches—all situations—are devalued by the abuser. When you have been told repeatedly for months and/or years that what you say is not important, you tend to compartmentalize and stuff down your experiences. Right now, I want you to decide to no longer do this.

Values are discussed frequently in mental health treatment, and most of us have heard how important it is to live according to ours. As a counselor and educator, I have learned many things over the years, but one stands out: we often derive our values from our moral compass, including our religious or spiritual beliefs. Consider that these values are not good or bad—they just are. By this I mean that each person has their own set of values, and thus, we cannot judge our values against the measure of other individuals' values. The narcissist in your life may try to convince you that their values are the only (or the most meaningful) ones, and has likely demanded that you live by them. But you no longer need to do that. It is very important that you take some time to assess values you hold in your life. So what are values? There are many ways to define them based on varying professional and personal perspectives. For the purpose of this chapter, I prefer to reference how acceptance and commitment therapy (ACT) explores values. This modality emphasizes that values are choices—specifically, the choices a person makes in their doing and being behaviors (Hayes et al., 2016). Stop for a minute to answer these questions:

- What do you choose to do regularly?
- What drives these behaviors?
- Regarding your sense of being, who do you want to be in your life?
- How do you want others to see you?

These are important questions because up until now, you have likely living according to the NPD abuser's values without even knowing it. Why? Narcissists see others in their lives as extensions of them. They believe you should do what they do, you should think what they think. That is why folks exposed to NPD abuse often feel a loss of identity, as I noted earlier in this book. When you step out of that influence, it is important that you stop and make a clear assessment of what you value. The first step is to reflect on what you are currently doing; then consider what you want to focus your "doing" on in the future so you can "be" your authentic self. After that you should take some time to examine a few other things, mentioned below, so you can get an idea of what your values are.

What do you spend most of your time doing? What we spend most of our time doing reflects what we value in our life. My behavior shows that I value family, work, exercise, pottery, writing, animals, and work. It is helpful to ask about our preferred activities instead of our values, as it is quite common for folks to *think* they have certain values rather than to acknowledge the reality of where they spend their time. Asking you to consider what you spend most of your time doing creates a shift from aspirational values to real values. I hope this helps you begin to see a starting point when considering your values.

The next level involves considering various areas in your life that you see as important for who you want to be. Oftentimes, we think about these areas of life from a broader perspective, as opposed to the narrower focus needed for personal assessment. We think in broader terms of careers, social life, community involvement, and being married or single. When we narrow our focusing on values, we may include our own marriage/intimate relationships, creativity, community, social relationships, physical health, spirituality/religion, parenting, education, mental health, and well-being. After reading this list, ask yourself, Where do I put most of my energy?

While examining this list of potential values, write down the ones where you put most of your energy. Next, it is imperative to put those in order from the most amount of time spent to the least amount of time. This reveals where your energy, or effort, is. If you wrote down something not listed, consider whether it may fall under any of the items/categories listed earlier. If not, then add that as a new value in your life. Now that you are aware of your current time priorities based upon your chosen order, you can begin to shuffle and reconsider.

Where do you want to intentionally put your energy? Once this is answered, focus on that one area. You do not have to adjust them all right away; in fact, you need to start with reshuffling just one before you can tackle more. Realistically, you may not be able to adjust to them, or you might be happy with where your values already are. However, if you are putting your energy where your abuser wants it, but not where you want it, then you are not living according to your values. Knowing what your values are as well as your current priorities helps you navigate future decisions for adjusting those priorities, leading you to validate the experiences you have within these various categories of values. This is important because you might be beating yourself up that your values have not been where you've truly wanted them to be. Remember, your NPD abuser has likely shaped your values so they can mold you into what they want. If someone has molded and shaped you, they want you to remain as they left you, like a finished piece of designed clay a potter leaves behind. But once the potter has finished the piece, you need to destroy how they molded it and make the piece how you would like it. If the clay is still wet, you can reshape it; if the piece has dried, you can break it, wet it, and then start over with your own design.

E: Exploring Other Aspects of Your Life Story

You no longer must stay in the mold that was created for you; you are now able to E, explore other aspects of your life story. You have assessed your values and are in the process of living according to those values. By doing this, you are slowly pulling away from your NPD abuser's grasp and are thinking and expanding your view beyond the narcissist's beliefs. The narcissist has likely been the central story in your life. It is time to explore other aspects of your life that extend beyond the NPD abuser. If I asked you to share your best or worst memory, it is probable that in doing so, you find both relate to the narcissist. But I would venture to say that some of the good stories of your life came before or even in spite of the NPD abuser in your life. For me, there were good and bad memories connected to my exposure, as I noted in Chapter 1. I am not asking you to consider other aspects of your life story so you can bash the narcissist but to provide you an opportunity to consider other narratives in your life that may have taken a back seat. In narrative therapy (White, 2007), counselors use a method of treatment that encourages the client to tell their story, which reinforces that individuals are the experts in their lives. In line with this therapy ideal, I encourage you to take out the stories that involve the narcissist, then put together a narrative of stories from your life. These are typically aligned to people, places, accomplishments, disappointments, opportunities, events, and special moments. To do this, think of your life like a time line from your birth until the present day. This can be easily accomplished when you take out a piece of paper, write out this time line, and do some free thinking. See what unfolds over the next 15 to 20 minutes. This can take some time, so you can start and stop, come back to it, or do one story at a time. Sometimes, once we start writing, it can be hard to stop because we get into the creative mindset. I would urge you to stop at 20 minutes and then reflect on what you have written. Examine at least one story that stands out as a memory not associated with your NPD abuser. After you have reflected upon this story, go back to that piece of paper, and answer a few questions.

- What emotions emerged while writing and then re-reading the story?
- What aspects of the story demonstrate a trait(s) about yourself that you really like?
- What aspects of the story demonstrate a trait(s) about yourself that frustrates you?
- Is there anything you would change about the story? If so, what would it be?

At this point you might be wondering about the purpose of this activity. Sometimes, you can get so bogged down with the needs, wants, and stories of the NPD abuser that you forget you have a separate identity and personality, with different experiences and behaviors. By considering events in your life not connected with your abuser, you can see how you have handled situations in the past and take note of the joys, sorrows, and even the average, peaceful moments.

N: Navigating the Elements of a New Identity

You can begin to N, navigate a new identity and make plans for change. In fact, the very nature of this reminiscence technique allows you a glimpse into your identity and even the chance to reflect upon the plans you had in the past or the desires you have for the future—without the influence of the narcissist. While considering your new identity, you might really want your old self or identity back. After your experience with the abuser, you are changed, and your identity thus is a version of your old self before it can be formulated into a new identity.

Another beneficial clinical theory to reference and use is Gestalt therapy, which focuses on the whole aspect of a person (Perls, 1992). I often think of it as a holistic approach to an individual, including who they are mentally, physically, emotionally, spiritually, and psychologically. This involves different parts of self: roles you play in your life and how you engage with people in the world. Additionally, it challenges you to focus on the present versus the past. You might think that you have been influenced so heavily by your NPD abuser that you can't function any other way. This is both true and untrue. I want you to realize that the person or role that you play and the behaviors you exhibit within the NPD relationship are only a part of who you are. These are the parts of you that help you survive. If you reflect upon this, you might get frustrated or wish you could do things differently. However, realistically, we all do the best we can, and it is very hard to get out of the cycle of focusing on and pleasing the NPD abuser. Nevertheless, it is important to remember that you may not know you can function differently until you have been shown a new way and have support for that change. Can you offer this part of yourself compassion and gratitude for doing the best you can? If you had a friend going through a similar situation, would you offer them compassion? Typically, it is much easier to empathize with others than it is with ourselves. I know as a counselor, I can offer compassion and support for others, but I am harder on myself.

Think of other parts of yourself that extend beyond the partner, friend, child, or colleague of a narcissist who must follow their rules. You have considered other stories that extend beyond the narcissist, and now it is important to consider elements of your identity that are separate from the narcissist's. What other parts of you may be hidden or muted? If you found this book, then a hidden part may be beginning to blossom. There is something about the relationship with the narcissist that you are beginning to question and maybe consider as not healthy for you.

Part of Gestalt therapy, beyond focusing on a holistic perspective, is embracing all versions of self as part of that holistic perspective. Let me give you an example from my own experience as a client. I was asked by a colleague to participate in a Gestalt session. As I sat with her, I told her I was frustrated about not speaking up to a colleague who treated me disrespectfully. I was avoiding confrontation. Before I was even aware of it, the colleague leading the session asked me to empathize with that part of myself and to reflect upon how that part of myself is useful in my life. Then she urged me to reflect upon the characteristics I prefer to use more often. I expressed my desire to be assertive and strong, not fearful. She challenged me to consider that both the avoidant and the assertive parts of myself are valid parts of who I am. I need those varied parts of self at different times in my life. She emphasized the importance of accepting self while highlighting how the avoidant part had both helped and hindered me. This additional reflection helped me realize that the part I desired to show, assertiveness, can be taught to emerge more often with practice.

After this session I had a lot of time to reflect and journal my thoughts. It was empowering to consider that there are varied qualities within myself that I use, and they emerge when and if they are needed. These parts are two of many that make up who I am, for I am also a wife, mother, counselor, educator, creative thinker, and friend. And all these roles have characteristics aligned to assist with my daily living. Accepting all these roles as part of a united front has helped me plan who I want to be: an authentic person. I know from my work as an educator that acquiring knowledge is not enough; it's important to take this knowledge and apply it. Ask yourself, How does understanding parts of who I am help me navigate a new identity and plan out steps to change? From my own perspective, I'd say it helps you validate that you have acquired the skills needed to function within a volatile environment based on what you've seen and experienced within the NPD relationship. You took that learning and responded in a way that helped you survive. Now you can rely on this new knowledge and other parts within you to make a plan for change and to respond differently.

T: Time Out to Reflect, Understand Your Past, and Reinvent Yourself

Give yourself permission to take T, time out to reflect. Each person is very different. Some folks will take new information and then impulsively make a decision, while others will sit on new information far too long and get stuck in the decision-making process. To effectively plan and make decisions, you should make a conscious effort to take a reasonable amount of time for reflecting. When reflecting, you are drawing from your thoughts, emotions, behaviors, and interactions. I am one of those people who can make quick decisions. However, I have learned to take time to reflect through practicing mindfulness and meditation so that I can delve deeper, beyond the information, to explore my next steps. Historically, when I have made an impulsive decision, I typically have regretted it. However, taking time to step away and delve into what I consider my intuitive self has been a useful tool in decision-making.

U: Understanding the Past and the Lessons Learned to Navigate a New Future

By taking this time, you can learn to U, understand your past and the lessons learned to begin to consider you future orientation. How do you do this? I have been successful with taking at least a day, preferably several days, to take some specific steps in self-evaluating. I tell my counselor-education students that when they get stuck and are unsure of next steps, they should pause, breathe, and proceed. This can be accomplished within a few intentional minutes by applying the steps to varied aspects of your life.

Pausing can initially look like literally getting quiet; removing your phone, television, or other auditory distractions; and being intentionally focused in the moment. I find it useful to be in a specific place, such as my office, with a sign that reads "Do not disturb" on my door, or in my bed, with my journal beside me and the door closed. Once I am at that place of pause, I typically close my eyes and take a deep belly breath. As I breathe in, I ask myself what I need to understand about the situation or decision. I exhale, then write down what emerges from my thoughts or even any images that might emerge in my mind's eye. I do this inhaling and exhaling for a few minutes so that I can get in a semirelaxed state. After the final exhale, I write down what has emerged, then I reflect upon what I have written down, which helps me to proceed further with my next step—typically, a decision. It might be about a job, a project, a relationship, or another issue that has arisen. I have done this practice when professional and personal issues arise. I used this method after my cancer diagnosis and during my treatment. We need a deeper understanding of where we have come from to take steps to a new beginning. This creates the space to start over.

R: Reinventing Yourself

I have heard individuals say it is too late to reinvent themselves, but I have found it is never too late. I've had middle-aged students decide to return to college, start new careers, and even change partners. Years ago, I encountered the concept of the individual's assertive bill of rights from the work of Manuel Smith (1975). There are several assertive rights, but a couple in particular resonated with me: "You have the right to change your mind," and "You have the right to say No and not feel guilty" (Smith, 1975). For the purpose of this book, I would add that "You have the right to reinvent myself." We may worry that our own people-pleasing tendencies will result in our poor decision-making, as we may not allow ourselves to make changes for fear of what others think. The potential consequences of changing our minds, standing up for ourselves, or inventing a new reality can be reinvigorating. The possibilities for reinventing oneself are endless. I urge you to reflect on the following: If you could change one thing to help reinvent yourself right now, what would it be?

E: Experiencing a New Life

As you reflect upon this, consider how this will be a catalyst for E, experiencing a new life. When I consider that I can—and have—experienced a new way of life, I realize I'd never have thought it possible when I was younger. The phrase "We have one life to live" has been reiterated for generations, but sadly, we often have limitations around this life. With each choice we make, there is a domino effect, acting on what comes afterward. Think about all the movies you've seen, books you've read, and testimonies you've heard from folks who talked about turning their lives around. Someone loses a loved one and decides to sell their house and move away, or there is a disaster, and the survivor decides to change careers. During December we see *The Grinch* and *A Christmas Carol*, two movies that depict the transformation of greedy, angry, and uncaring individuals into loving, giving, and empathetic characters. You may have hoped for this in your own relationship with your NPD abuser, but this hope was fleeting and was not fulfilled. Remember that the steps you are taking in this book are for *you*. You no longer need to wait for the narcissist to change, because the likelihood of that happening is slim, but *you* can decide to begin experiencing a new life. The new-life experience can happen now, and it is, in fact, inevitable after you've completed the various reflections and actions outlined so far in this book. Now you can begin to venture and implement some regular practices in your life to reinforce the new you.

Let's recap what has unfolded in the book so far. You have explored NPD, you have captured a glimpse into my own story of NPD abuse, and you hopefully feel a sense of resonation and validation regarding the impact of NPD abuse. Starting the healing process has taken you through the importance of self-assessment, finding MEANING from the experience, beginning to EVOLVE, and now you are beginning to VENTURE into the experience of a new you. All of these are processes to help you build your strength, resilience, and tools to become your authentic self. As we continue into the second half of this book, you will learn specific skills to implement in your daily life to maintain the healing.

Prior to closing out this chapter, I think it is important to take you on a mini journey so you can picture yourself venturing into the unknown. Please read this passage, and take some time to reflect upon the questions.

Imagine it is a perfect sunny day with spring temperatures. Flowers are blooming, the sky is blue, the sound of wind and birds fill the air, and you decide to go on a stroll through a field of blooming daisies to set up a picnic on the other side. Ordinarily, you would have a companion with you, but for some reason, on this day, you felt an urge to go alone. You are walking and taking in all of the beauty around you. As you get to the edge of the field of daisies, you see that there are three paths in front of you. In your memory, there was only one path, but today you see three. You feel a sense of wonder, asking yourself where each could take you, and there are no signs to direct you where to go. Also, you feel a bit of anxiety, for you want to take the right path, but there is no way to know which one is the best. However, you assume they will all get you to a destination where you can have your picnic. Now consider these three paths as part of your psychological venture into the unknown of your healing from NPD abuse.

What do each of these three paths/choices represent for you and your choices as you venture?

1. Path one:

   _____

   _____

2. Path two:

   _____

   _____

3. Path three:

   _____

   _____

What could happen if you take a path and it does not turn out how you imagined?

_____

_____

_____

What steps could you take if you reinvent yourself, then turn around on a path that's a dead end to try another? Remember that we can always turn around and try another.

_____

_____

_____

What could happen if you take a path, and it turns out to be exactly what you were expecting?

_____

_____

_____

Explain how you would know that this was the path for you.

_____

_____

_____

There is always the option to turn back around, to cross the daisy-laden field, and to go back where you came from. But I often remind myself that while going back to an old way of knowing may seem safe, it can be a death to self. Once we are aware of new information, a new knowing, we cannot pretend that we do not know what we know. Our bodies desire to venture further and make choices.

CHAPTER 7

~

Learning Mindfulness

Mindfulness has been explored across Buddhism, Hinduism, and yoga practices beginning in the East. The movement of mindfulness was brought to the West by Jon Kabat-Zinn, who trained in the method under several Buddhist teachers. Kabat-Zinn found mindfulness so influential in his own life that he desired to share his knowledge surrounding the method with individuals in the West. As a result, he founded the Center for Mindfulness at the University of Massachusetts Medical School. There he developed the Mindfulness-Based Stress Reduction (MBSR) program, which many helping professionals apply in both their client work and personal use for stress reduction. I know that in my own life, mindfulness has been a helpful tool enabling me to stay in the here and now and manage stress.

To learn the skill of mindfulness, you must not only conceptualize the definition but learn to effectively apply its tenets within your life. As we delve into this chapter, we explore the definition coined by Jon Kabat-Zinn. Then we explore practicing mindfulness and how it can help both cognitively and emotionally. This practice includes various methods of application, and it is likely you will prefer one method over others. Knowing the different methods will not only help you understand how and why to practice mindfulness, but it can also help you reduce the pitfalls resulting from a relationship with an NPD abuser. This chapter provides some practical tools to be applied in your daily life.

When you hear the word mindfulness, what do you think of? This term has been used frequently over the last 20 years. Not only has it been discussed in the context of mental health treatment, but it has been applied in yoga studios, corporate offices, high school classes, in retreat workshops, and so forth. I want us to go beyond merely utilizing mindfulness as a trend; I'd love for it to be something easy you can apply in your life. My hope is that you leave the practice feeling revived and at peace. So let's define it. This is another area where many folks have varied perspectives. I prefer to draw directly from Jon Kabat-Zinn. He defined mindfulness as "paying attention in a particular way: on purpose, in the present moment, and nonjudgmentally" (Kabat-Zinn, 1994, p. 4). Breaking down this definition is helpful because it can easily come across as a philosophical rather than a practical practice. Paying attention takes effort, as it requires one to be able to intentionally focus and switch their attention as the experience unfolds. It can be a challenge, but the more you practice, the easier it becomes to pay attention with purpose. The skill of considering the present moment is connected to your awareness of your moment-to-moment experience, which is absorbed when you practice a mindfulness skill. I often remind myself to get out of my head and get into the present. We cannot shut off our thinking, but we can redirect our thinking and attention back to where we intended it to be. We are also instructed to be nonjudgmental, which refers to releasing the automatic judgments that arise as we are within our mindfulness exercise. We as humans will judge, and as an NPD abuse survivor, you are used to being judged. Thus, you are likely used to thinking ahead, planning ways to avoid others' judgment being cast on you. Consider letting go of the automatic judgments that arise in your mind. Consider practicing the following quick mindfulness exercise:

Take 2 minutes to breathe deeply. As you inhale through your nose, count to five, then pause. On the exhale, breathe out through your mouth while you slowly count to five. Repeat these steps for 2 minutes.

Now I would like for you to write down the automatic judgments that came to your mind:

_____

_____

_____

In addition to the automatic judgments you wrote, I would like for you to decide whether these judgments are good, bad, or neutral. Sometimes, I hear common judgments such as "I am not good at this" or "I feel silly." We all have judgments, and yet we need to understand the importance of accepting the present moment without judgment; the more you practice, the easier you will find redirecting your thoughts. In fact, mindfulness helps improve our awareness of when our mind has wandered, to recognize that the thoughts are there, and that we can return our attention to our intended purpose.

It is important to distinguish between mindfulness and meditation. Mindfulness is very mobile and can be applied anywhere, at any time, whereas "meditation is a practice where an individual uses a technique—such as mindfulness or focusing the mind on a particular object, thought, or activity—to train attention and awareness, and achieve a mentally clear and emotionally calm and stable state" (Shapero et al., 2018, p. 32). This definition contains a lot of information, but it can be broken down as follows: simply, meditation is one method for learning to live mindfully, and mindfulness is only one aspect of meditation.

Why Is Mindfulness Important?

Consider what you have been through with your NPD abuser. Realistically, the person has been training you to think, believe, and speak in compliance with all their requests. You can look at them across the room and, from their facial expressions and demeanor, know that they are pleased or displeased with you; this makes it your job to constantly be in your head, attempting to predict their moods and the next "right" steps. This disapproval could be connected to anything: politics, religion, others' opinions, their competence, and/or your incompetence. Whether we want to believe it or not, this is not only mind control but mind training. When you are brainwashed long enough, not unlike in a cult, you believe what you are told. It can be very difficult to rewire your thinking and subsequent behavior. All you know is what you were told, and you learn to comply, keep your head down, walk on eggshells, and engage in future forward thinking. I have often found that my skill of future forward thinking has been both a blessing and a curse. I know curse is a strong word, but it does feel that way. Let me explain. Due to my years of experiencing NPD abuse, I became a pro at predicting my mother's mood. I could tell by the look in her face and eyes, by her tone of voice and demeanor, what I needed to do. I had to carefully consider my own words, behavioral responses, and plans of action to survive. Yes, sometimes my only survival mechanism was walking on eggshells. I know I use this term a lot, but literally, I had to be very careful with everything I said, sometimes remaining quiet and tiptoeing around interactions as if eggshells had been laid out and I had to navigate around them. The blessing of this is that I am now good at mediating aggressive situations and can de-escalate people. In fact, I have been told many times how calm and positive I remain during stressful and overwhelming situations within my clinical and professorial work. Of course, I do not tell those people that I had years of practice.

Even as a young child, I was in my head a lot. I would consider the potential reaction of my mother, father, and siblings—even of my sexual abuser—and it would often save me from harm. I would think about where to sit in my house; when to go to my bedroom; when to appease; when to lie; when to ask a question about friends, school, or activities; and when I had to out-manipulate the manipulator. I never knew I was doing this, as it was simply a way of life, but now, as an adult, I've come to understand narcissism and my methods of coping. There were times I would feel bad for the ways I was acting, but not thinking ahead meant more verbal and emotional abuse and isolation. I must remind myself that I did not know any other way of being; I did it for my own sanity.

Today, these skills help me a great deal as a counselor who can not only educate about this topic but who can spot both a narcissist and a survivor. It has helped enhance my radar for people who may not be good for me personally. It has helped me mediate with couples and families, manage conflicts between students (or between a student and I), analyze situations, research, and I am good at putting physical and figurative pieces together in a more organized way. It also means that I can spot a lie, and though I hate when people lie, I also have compassion for them, as I understand why folks do it. I've worked with individuals who have lied as a way of saving themselves. I can relate to this when I remember how, as a child, I lied to my mother when she asked me if I ate lunch at school. I said yes even when I had not, because I knew she would yell and scream at me, telling me that I was anorexic if I admitted I'd not eaten. I could not rationalize with her and say I was not hungry because I was still full from the huge breakfast she'd made me eat. So the best thing for me to do was lie. And this leads to why this is a curse.

Future forward thinking can be a curse due to possibility of misreading. I was so accustomed to my manipulative mother that I assume all folks, especially women, are manipulative. If someone paid me a compliment, told me a story, or said they were going to do something, I did not believe them. I would consider their ulterior motive, look for the gap in the story, and wait for them to fail me. Yes, sometimes this did happen, but there were good people who meant what they said and who proved trustworthy over time. I would be in conversations with these people, ruminating about what they'd said, what I should have said, and second-guessing the actions I should have taken; this was all so immense that it would sometimes bring me to tears and lead me to self-isolate. In other words, forward thinking was useful in the relationship with a narcissist, but I could not continue to live my life questioning everyone's motives, not trusting women (and even men), keeping myself guarded from relationships, and judging others' intentions based on the experiences in my life. Also, part of my experience with future thinking is that I could be an intense people pleaser. I would think ahead about what the person might want, whether it involved seeing a friend, going out to eat, or work projects. I took on too much work and organizing and planning of projects, and though this would sometimes help me, at other times, it backfired. I became a perfectionist, which I still battle, even though it has improved tremendously over the years. I often remember that in chaotic family environments, the only always-predictable dynamic is that family behavior is unpredictable. This statement likely needs to sink in a little, as it can be confusing. In other words, once a pattern is finally set within a dysfunctional family, it will change. I would always have to adjust and adapt, then figure out the new pattern. It is a lot of work.

Now that I have shared the types of coping skills I learned from NPD abuse, consider what you learned from NPD abuse exposure. This may take some time to reflect upon, but it is critical so that you can figure out what thoughts, emotions, and behaviors you need to adjust. This will also help you set your intention as you begin practicing mindfulness. Take 5 minutes to reflect.

_____

_____

_____

_____

_____

I want to get back to why I practice mindfulness. Since narcissists have practiced mind control over us, our exercising of mindfulness comes into play in a powerful way. As a contemplative practice, mindfulness has been utilized for centuries. According to Dahl and Davidson, "contemplative practices may thus be defined as efforts that promote human flourishing by training the mind" (2019, p. 60). Ample evidence indicates that training the mind via mindfulness is beneficial to our mental health because it can assist us with observing a situation rather than attaching to our negative thoughts (cognitive thinking ahead) about it. When we approach our thoughts in a nonjudgmental way, we reduce the likelihood that our emotional reactions will lead to potential long-term behavioral responses. I have found that mindfulness practices that aligned to my personality were beneficial in dealing with some of my unhealthy patterns, and now I hope that since you have assessed yours, you can implement some of these practices and see results that greatly benefit you.

Implementing Mindfulness

Before you implement mindfulness, it is important you know the varied types of mindfulness practices that could benefit you and other individuals healing from NPD abuse. Many individuals across varied paradigms have created different methods of mindfulness that they apply in everyday life. There were many folks fortunate enough to study under Jon Kabat-Zinn, and they found profound benefits to how he illuminated mindfulness practice. Thus, they took his ideas and brought them to numerous places: mental health and medical facilities, yoga studios, and even corporate settings. If you search any online or physical setting where books are sold, you will see many books on mindfulness and meditation, which grew from these roots. These skills are drawn from many different influences and researchers.

What Skills

The "what" skills of mindfulness include the use of observing, describing, and participating with awareness (Linehan, 2015). In this section, I take you through each of these skills and then provide you an opportunity to practice them. The first skill is the "what" skill called observing. We use the observing skill every day. We might take a walk on a spring day and see the sun shining and flowers budding, but does that mean we are truly observing? With observing, it is important to consider paying attention *on purpose*. To do this as you walk on a spring day, you might look up and observe the sun and the flowers, but you must walk with no music, smart phone, or other distractions. In a world of multitasking, observing asks you to do one thing at a time and notice the reality right in front of you. Considering the use of your five senses is an observing technique that falls under the first "what" skill.

Stop reading for a few minutes, and take notice of what you are experiencing through your five senses: seeing, hearing, smelling, tasting, and touching. One way to practice this skill is to choose your favorite candy or chocolate. After you have selected the chocolate or candy, observe the candy as you hold it. What does it feel like? What does it look like? What does the sound of the wrapper sound like? You merely need to observe with your touch, sight, and hearing. Now open the piece of candy and smell it. What does it smell like? Does it look different now that it is out of the wrapper? Now taste it. Put it in your mouth, and do not eat it right away; feel the texture on your tongue, and then slowly chew it. All this observing through your senses might potentially stimulate your thoughts, emotions, and body sensations. This five-sense activity all depends upon what you focus your attention on at the moment. It can be many different things, so consider what things you could observe with your senses. When you observe, do not react, label, or describe your thoughts—just experience them. If you labeled the candy in your mind or made judgments, go back and observe it again.

The second "what" skill is describing. It is important for you to understand the importance of observing before we delve into describing. Why? It is not possible to describe something that you have not observed through your five senses. When we describe, we are actually attaching words to specific experience—for example, consider you are eating a piece of candy that you describe in your mind as tasting sour. You may think, "I do not want to eat this." If you were to apply the describing technique beyond the observing-candy exercise and use it in an interaction with your NPD abuser, it would be important to consider the gravity of labeling what you observe as it is: a thought is just a thought, a feeling is just a feeling, and an action is just an action. It is essential that you do not apply meaning to it. I know this can be a hard skill (it was for me) because it forces you to not overanalyze but rather to tell yourself, "I am having a thought right now," and "I am having a feeling right now," versus "I need to not think this," "I should be thinking this," or "Ignore your emotions, and just move on." We NPD abuse survivors are accustomed to interpreting and then taking action based upon our inter-pretation. In fact, this makes another describing skill even more challenging. This skill asks us to pull away from interpretations and opinions and focus on the facts, which include what we observe: the who, what, when, and where. You can think of these like a statement from a lawyer or a judge, who tell you to just focus on the facts. These describing skills, used at various times, help you focus on the understanding that not every thought is fact.

We've been trained to believe what our NPD abuser would say, and thus, our thoughts have been trained to please them and believe them. For example, let's say your NPD abuser has told you that you are crazy. You might think, "I am crazy!" But remember this method: check the facts. Just because your abuser says you are crazy, that does not mean you are. If, after years of abuse, you believe that you are ugly and unlovable, that does not mean that you are. We all deserve love. You are not unlovable. Imagine that you go out to dinner with a group of friends. One friend keeps whisper-ing to the other but not talking directly to you, while another one is looking at her phone, and another is eating, not talking to anyone. You begin to interpret their behaviors and jump to the conclusion that they are mad at you and do not like you, so you must be boring. With this unfolding, you have turned your observations into facts, which are possibly misinterpretations. But what if you merely described their actions? Your friends are doing various behaviors, such as looking at the phone, eating, and whispering to another. Those are the facts, and there is no need to interpret them any other way. You will be in less emotional pain when you describe than when you create your own perceptions (and overanalyze).

These are some practices that can assist you with being present. Exercises like these show you how to just describe situations so that, with enough practice, this skill can resonate when you are with other people.

1. Consider what you see outside of yourself. Sit in a café and describe what one of the staff is doing—make sure you don't attach intentions, outcomes, or judgments. For example, "The waitress is picking up my glass and walking to the bar, sorting through tickets, and clearing a table." This type of describing can be done while lying on the ground and looking up at the sky, sitting on a bench, or sitting at a park, at home, or in a library.
2. Consider describing thoughts and feelings that you are having. You can describe your feelings as they well up within you, such as the following: "A feeling of anxiety is developing in my chest."
3. Let's say you are sitting in a board meeting. You will describe your thoughts after your boss has said or done something. For example, "When my boss does this, I feel this."
   If you were just provided a promotion for your hard work, you might describe it this way:
   "Getting this raise, I feel appreciation for my efforts."

The last "what" skill is participating. We humans are quite accustomed to this. Have you ever been sitting at a sporting event, watching a movie, playing a video or board game, dancing, singing, or doing a craft, and you got lost in that moment? It feels good to be out of your thoughts and in the present moment. We often engage life in a state of autopilot, but when we practice participatory mindfulness, we can experience the joy of participating or experiencing an activity. When considering this "what" skill, I like to ask myself, What are you doing to be present? I have found that participation practices are often easy for individuals to implement in their lives, but the key word here is *intentionality* with the participation, as well as trying to not multitask.

Have you ever been with someone at an event like bowling or playing cards? You can insert any activity. These are activities that require concentration, but you notice that the other person is on their phone while playing; maybe they are distracted by what is going on around them? Maybe they're multitasking? This might, in fact, be you. Well, if you are only there for one purpose, in the down moments (such as waiting your turn during a game), it may be quite easy to do other things. But why not just bowl or just play cards? When we allow ourselves to be distracted or seek to have multiple activities, we can miss out on the fun and joy that arises in the present moment.

When choosing participation activities, consider what you enjoy spending your time doing. For me, I love to work out at the gym (cardio and weights), watch crime television, listen to podcasts, play board games with my family, cook, write, throw pottery on the wheel, glaze pottery, garden, and journal. Take a moment to ask yourself, What do I like to do for enjoyment? Maybe you appreciate watching or attending a sporting event, taking a bath, drawing, watching a program on television, or reading a good book. Write those down so you can determine how to use one of these activities to practice participatory mindfulness.

_____

_____

_____

_____

I hope these practices have successfully demonstrated how you can practice participatory mindfulness. Once you have chosen an activity, throw yourself completely into it—or another activity—by doing it in the present moment. To effectively accomplish this, it is important that you do not multitask, which separates you from what is going on at that moment. If you are watching a sporting event, focus on the game and allow yourself to get lost in that activity.

Another method is to become one with what you are doing. For example, if you are sculpting clay, allow yourself to get lost in sculpting. If your mind wanders to your phone or another distraction, redirect it right back to the sculpting. I know when I throw on my pottery wheel, I lose track of time because I am so focused in those moments, which is very relaxing and peaceful.

In some situations, like when you are at work, participating involves just doing what you need to do in the position you are in at the time, not thinking ahead too much or getting stuck and then doing nothing. I find this helps me not be anxious about what is to come and focus on what I actually am doing.

How Skills

The "how" skills of mindfulness reinforce taking a nonjudgmental stance with an intentional focus on one thing at a time (Linehan, 2015). When we consider how this set of mindfulness skills is utilized, we must understand the components of this definition. We explored nonjudgment earlier in this chapter, but with the "how" skills, we learn exactly how to practice mindfulness. Linehan (2015) broke down these skills into three broad categories, including practicing being nonjudgmental, practicing one-mindfully, and practicing effectively. This section examines the breakdown of these skills and provide examples of how to implement them. But first, let's answer why we need to practice the "how" skills. This set of skills is considered the guide to effectively learning how to manage emotions, handle distress, and manage relationships.

Category 1: Nonjudgmental Skills

It is very common, especially in the context of an NPD abusive relationship, to apply judgments to what we observe in our daily lives. We may have been taught to judge situations and adapt ourselves based on the narcissist's wants, or maybe their psychological abuse taught us to constantly judge ourselves. Being constantly in our heads, judging, can lead to unhealthy emotions, such as shame, guilt, sadness, and anger. What is a judgment? A judgment happens when we attach an opinion or perspective to an observation. I encourage you to ask yourself, When do I pass the most judgment on myself or others? Is it during a certain time of day or event, when you are with a particular person, or when you are doing a specific task?

To achieve being nonjudgmental, consider taking a metaphorical step back to see what is happening in the moment; focus on just the facts. Part of this mindfulness practice includes the following:

1. Accept each moment as it is with the knowledge that you have no control over the moment.
2. Acknowledge your thoughts, emotions and experiences without assigning them a label or trying to evaluate them.

3. Judging your ability to practice being nonjudgmental needs to stop: "When you find yourself judging, don't judge your judging" (Linehan, 2015, p. 60).

Category 2: One-Mindfully Skills

We have addressed the concept of being in the present moment. With one-mindfully skills, individuals should focus on the present moment, not unlike with participatory mindfulness; however, this practice particularly helps with enhancing your awareness. These skills include the following:

1. Doing one thing at a time. If you are eating, eat. If you are reading, read. Think about something you like to do, and practice only doing that. I have done this with walking. I only walk without distraction: without listening to music, talking on the phone, or walking with a partner.
2. If your thoughts trail off to other things while you're doing this activity, take your mind back to what you were doing. So if you are walking and your phone rings, allow the phone to ring, then get back to walking. If your thoughts start going to a work project, redirect and get back to what you are doing: walking.
3. If you are doing two or three other things, stop yourself and go back to doing the one thing.

Category 3: Practicing Effectively

When we think of effectiveness, we may ask ourselves, How can I be effective in implementing mindfulness? Remind yourself that you do not know which of the mindfulness skills will be effective for you until you actually try them. In order to choose which works for you, first consider your goals, then anticipate how your choice in skills can assist you with achieving those goals. You might find that you practice one mindfulness skill more than another. Remember to not judge yourself for this, because being effective includes doing what works for you, not avoiding an activity. Consider that it is good to use whichever skill you need at the time. If you are experimenting with the different skills, then you are being effective.

Given your experiences with an NPD abuser, you will likely find that writing a narrative of an event is an effective skill to help you implement these skills into your experiences. What sets this approach apart from journaling is that you will write out a specific event from your day (or a previous day) with detailed step-by-step aspects of what happened. Think of it like a recipe, but you not only share what unfolded in your environment, you outline what your thoughts, feelings, and behaviors were. The key to this activity is that you need to omit your judgment regarding why something happened or why you thought, felt, or behaved a certain way. Stick with the facts.

In the midst of the NPD abusive relationship, we experienced countless times when we wanted our opinions heard, even though we realistically knew that this would not happen, as there is no changing the narcissist. Linehan (2015) developed what she coined a STOP skill for assisting individuals with interrupting their typically reactive responses. This mindfulness skill reminds us to take a moment before proceeding with what we want to say. Please stop what you are doing right now and complete the steps below.

S: Stop your thoughts, emotions, and whatever behavior you are engaging by pausing.
T: Take a purposeful deep breath; deeply inhale and then exhale.
O: Use your mindful observing skill to acknowledge what is happening at the moment, as well as your thoughts and feelings, without judgment.
P: You can now proceed mindfully because you have taken this pause and can be intentional versus reactive about the response.

Since this is a simulated activity, you may not experience an authentic response to conducting this STOP technique, but I encourage you to apply this activity in at least one real-life situation to see how it assists you. Taking that pause provides you the space to consider your response based upon your goals.

Mindfulness Fit

We have explored the history of mindfulness—the purpose and benefits—and then divided them specifically into "what" skills and "how" skills. Additionally, we integrated specific ways to apply these skills and decided to apply the skills that are most useful for us. There are many activities for applying mindfulness in our daily lives, which years of research has made available. As I noted, you can purchase mindfulness books or listen to mindfulness guided imagery online or on your smartphone, but whatever platform is used, it is critical to think about finding the right fit for mindfulness in your life. My exposure to narcissism taught me to ignore my feelings, preferring logical thinking. I found it never helped to express my emotions to my mother, and in fact, I felt she had enough emotions to go around, so it was better for me to stay quite logical. But once I left home, my emotions overcame me as though I were drowning in the flood. Since I'd held so much in for so long, my body had to release some of it to cut the pressure. But later in life, when I stepped back and evaluated my experience, I realized my emotions came from a sense of guilt where I never felt good enough for my mom, as well as a sense of loss for what I would never receive: her approval.

As a clinician and educator, I often talk about the ways we might react to the world around us. Do you tend to react with your head or your heart? The approach of facing situations from the heart (emotion center) or from the head (cognitive center) seems to resonate with individuals. Think about making decisions in your life and how you typically react. Do you typically go with your emotions or feelings (heart), or do you cognitively (head) process and go with the most logical answer? Does it have to be one or the other? Honestly, I used to fear that I was wrong to go with my emotional reaction when making decisions. However, after I would think through things focusing on the logical perspective, I'd find that, somehow, the most logical decision would often align with the emotional reaction I was experiencing. Realistically, life does not always work that way, and sometimes we need to have a combination of both the head and the heart. We are human and have these abilities within us for a reason. Maybe this is what Linehan (2015) was considering when she talked about the importance of using our wise mind. Tapping into our wise mind might be the answer to balancing out life decisions. Linehan (2015) emphasized that individuals make decisions based on their reasonable mind and emotional mind, but that it is critical to teach folks a third choice: the use of their wise mind. Those who prefer to make decisions based upon a reasonable mind typically focus on facts, reason, logic, and pragmatics. Someone who makes decisions from their emotional mind is influenced by mood, feelings, and urges. And there is something lacking in choosing one over the other. That dearth of peace is the wise mind within each of us. Someone who makes decisions based upon their wise mind can recognize the wisdom in each person, values emotions *and* rational thinking, and sees the benefit of using both sides of the brain and bringing together the head and heart, as we have been exploring. So how do we tap into the wise mind? There are many ways that people choose to do this, but I have found when a situation arises, getting to my wise mind is easier when I have fewer distractions, have a piece of paper and pen, and can take 5 to 10 minutes for visualization.

Here is the script of the visualization I have been doing for several years.

Visualization

Sit in a chair, open your journal to a blank sheet, and with paper and pen, take down any reflections. Close your eyes, take about 1 minute to practice deep belly breaths by inhaling through your nose, and allow air to fill up your belly. Then you will exhale out of your mouth, allowing your belly to deflate and your shoulders to drop. Once you get into a rhythm of breathing, imagine that you are walking on a beautiful sunny day through a meadow. On the left of you is a stream of water glistening in the sun; you can hear the water flowing and see trees bordering the stream. There are beautiful daffodils leading up the path from the bank of the stream to where you are walking. As you turn your head forward, you see an old country-style home with a wraparound porch adorned with rocking chairs. In one of the rocking chairs sits an individual, who is rocking peacefully. There is a content and loving expression on the person's face. You turn your head to the right, and as you look, you see various individuals nearby, all whom seem familiar to you. Some of them are picking flowers, some are tilling the land and gardening, and some are setting up seats near a firepit, waiting for the sun to go down to sit around the fire. You are drawn to direct your gaze toward the house and the person rocking in the porch chair. As you walk toward the house, slow down your pace, and focus your eyes on the person rocking. You feel yourself more and more drawn to get to the house to reach this person. You walk to the front of the house, up the stairs, and to the porch, then direct your attention to the person sitting there. As you walk up to the rocking chair, you become immediately aware that the person is you. The resemblance is clear, but this is a wiser, more advanced entity than who you are currently. The person looks at you and says, "I know why you are here." At this point you sit down in the rocking chair that is directly in front of this person, and your eyes lock. You ask the question you've long been seeking an answer to. This person is your wise mind, a deeper part of you that offers you wisdom and the answers you are looking for, and they include the rational, emotional, and intuitive awareness that is within you. Allow yourself time to sit and reflect upon the answer they've given. You can ask one or more questions. There is no need to rush. Once you have your answers, offer thanks to that wise part of yourself, and journey back down the stairs, down the path. When you pause and turn to look back, the house and the person are now in the distance. Once you get back to the end of the path, where the meadow began, open your eyes and write in the journal the answers that were provided for you.

I have utilized this visualization many times in my life, and often, I find myself turning to it at least once a week. It is a journey that helps me balance my emotional and cognitive reaction. It moves me deeper into the core of myself when I need to make a decision or process an event. Now I would like you to try it for yourself. One thing I encourage you to do is to take your smartphone (or a similar device) and record yourself walking through this script so you can access it when you need it. Once you have listened to this a couple of times, it will be easy to visualize it. Or you might create your own version that leads you to a wise decision. After you have recorded the script, take some time to do the following:

1. Consider what question(s) you would like to ask your wise self, and write them down. I would encourage you to focus on your current or former NPD abuse experience. This will vary for each and every person due to the nature of the relationship. Maybe you want directions regarding next steps in the relationship or to reflect upon some of the information you have read so far in this book. Ponder at least one question.

_____

_____

_____

2. Get in a quiet location where you will not be distracted by noise, family, or friends.
3. Use your audio recorded script, close your eyes, and visualize what you hear on the recording.
4. After you have listened to the answers given by your wise self, or even while you are getting those answers, write them down.

_____

_____

_____

5. Practice this at least once a week to get into a regular practice routine to enhance your self-reflection and self-awareness.

As a counselor educator, I find it is imperative to be personally self-reflective and self-aware and to teach my students to practice these skills so they can enhance how they interact with others and grow their skills. So what are the skills associated with self-reflection and self-awareness? First, these are a choice. We have to make a specific effort to focus on our emotions, thoughts, feelings, and actions. We make these choices based upon our values and beliefs, which come from the influences in our lives, but these can be shifted when we are exposed to new experiences. Also, there are times in our lives where we are forced to self-reflect; these might be associated with a transition in life, such as a graduation, a new job, going to college, marriage, having children, experiencing a crisis, or even an illness. Whenever there are big shifts or notable events in our lives, we should reflect. However, it does not have to take a big crisis or transition for us to reflect; we can make an intentional effort to self-reflect, which this book strives to help you do. Self-reflection enhances self-awareness, which leads to new thoughts and, subsequently, new behaviors. Our thoughts influence our emotions, which trickle down to our behaviors and can be a powerful tool for change. Self-reflection thus promotes change because it enhances self-awareness while we are engaging with others across various areas of our lives, including in our relationships, work, spiritual/religious beliefs, and daily interactions (Demnitz-King et al., 2022). Individuals who are self-aware tend to be more cognizant and conscious of events, interactions, and influence. After reviewing this chapter regarding varied ways of implementing mindfulness, we also know there are multiple ways to enhance self-reflection and subsequent awareness. Having these skills can benefit you psychologically. Now is the time to practice our ability to enhance these skills when interacting with others.

CHAPTER 8

~

Relationship Building and Maintenance

Relationships are a part of all our lives. We experience numerous different types of relationships across our life span. We have parental, peer, familial, community, colleague, romantic, and acquaintance relationships. How we identify relationships depends upon our experiences. We discussed this in an earlier chapter when we explored our environmental influences and our attachment style. It can also depend upon our genetics—specifically, if we are more extroverted or introverted. Extroverts need and feel connected to individuals, and being social feeds their energy. They feel gratified when around others, as well as a true joy in community. Introverts are fine with being alone and prefer focusing on themselves. Being around other individuals saps their energy, and they need to decompress with some alone time, which restores thems (Petric, 2022). Of course, relationships cannot merely be defined from this narrow perspective, but this provides a framework for understanding interaction patterns and how these specific styles engage with others. Being either an introvert or an extrovert not only influences how one communicates but also how often and to what extent, which in turn influences how many relationships one gets involved in throughout their life. Involvement within relationships is both involuntary and voluntary. How can this be?

You are born into a family, and you have no choice about that family raising you—that environment is out of your control. Of course, children can be removed from that family and be given to another via adoption or foster care. Also, you are required to get an education and subsequently to either pursue work or a college to gain additional education. Your engagement within all of these systems is not voluntary. There are laws requiring school attendance, and parents/guardians often dictate attendance in extracurricular and community connections, including in religious institutions. Of course, once someone starts high school, college, or new employment, they can decide to stay or leave based upon the interactions and relationships they find there. Voluntary relationships are more commonly connected with the choice of friends, a partner, individuals within chosen hobbies, or other groups, such as religious communities. We feel connected to certain people, while we can feel disconnected to others. Sometimes, this is due to cultural similarities or differences, but there are other times when individuals clearly click as friends or as partners for a romantic relationship. In our minds, we all have our list of preferences for a relationship. They are often based upon our values and beliefs and, of course, the influence of others around us. If you were to step back and review your voluntary and involuntary relationships in your life, who would be included where? Why? Take a moment to reflect upon that in Table 8.1 below.

Not only do we often find ourselves in questionable relationships but we may also lack an imagination about what to look for in a relationship and then seek out individuals based upon specific familiar characteristics. You may be questioning yourself right now as you think about what you'd seen in your NPD abuser. Remember, NPD abusers are manipulative and lack empathy, so they can mimic the traits you desire for quite a while, pulling you in without your realizing it. They do quite a lot of love bombing, exhibiting love, affection, and interests similar to your own. Take a minute to complete Table 8.2 (if not as a parent, then as someone who would engage with children). Next, examine what characteristics you look for and are drawn to when it comes to friendships, work colleagues, and romantic partners.

Now that you have reviewed your preferred relationship characteristics, I think it is important to consider how the relationship with your NPD abuser began and how it has impacted you. This is important to do before we delve into managing this individual as well as future relationships. As you review the table of characteristics you wrote for parents, friends, colleagues and romantic partners, consider the NPD abuser in your life and if

Table 8.1. Relationship Connections

Voluntary Relationships	Involuntary Relationships

Table 8.2. My Desired Relationship Characteristics

	Parent or Parent-Like	Friendships	Colleagues	Romantic Partner
Characteristics				

the characteristics you desired matched how this person really is/was with you. Consider the following areas for reflection.

Who is your NPD abuser (e.g., parent, friend, colleague, romantic partner)?

_____

_____

_____

What characteristics did they demonstrate when you first met them?

_____

_____

_____

Consider these characteristics, and write out which ones did and did not meet your expectations for a relationship. It is important to write these down.
Met:

_____

_____

_____

Did not meet:

_____

_____

_____

What made you begin to question this relationship and seek out additional help with understanding and managing it?

_____

_____

_____

I want you to step away from self-blame regarding this relationship. Even if we'd seen something that was not aligned to our desires, we might not have been able to leave, because it was a parent, partner, or supervisor. Also, it might have been very difficult to get out due to the nature of the relationship: there might have been real physical danger to you or someone you love, or maybe there was financial manipulation. It takes a lot of psychological and emotional skill and strength to not only find a way out but to figure out how to effectively manage such a relationship. You have already completed a lot of your own self-reflection and work thus far in this chapter, but there is more to explore. This chapter focuses on understanding what you as a survivor have learned about relationships and applying those skills to manage relationship choices in the future effectively. This includes application of communication skills, the process of maintaining healthy relationships, practicing authenticity to preserve self-respect, maintaining boundaries, and learning when and how to end destructive relationships.

You have likely evaluated your communication styles due to receiving judgment on how you do and do not communicate. As I delve into communication styles, I concentrate not on how others perceive you but on your own assessment of your style of communicating and encourage you to consider the way you express yourself with others. I have often said that we teach people how to treat us. This is not only true for you but for me as well. As I reflect on my own life, I recognize how I was trained early on that passivity and people-pleasing were the best ways to function effectively in my family. The problems began when I continued these same patterns in adulthood, which led to me beating myself up in many situations where I hadn't stood up for myself or felt like I was at fault for negative outcomes. Of course, I am not solely to blame for all problems, but I'd taken on this role, which was overwhelmingly difficult to handle as an adolescent. As I began to investigate my communication style, I came across information about communication patterns, which helped me understand my current style and goal of becoming more assertive. You may be wondering, Why is assertiveness the ultimate goal? In this section I explore the varied forms of communication and the importance of becoming assertive.

In the field of psychology, clinicians commonly explore communication with their clients. In fact, communication is a critical part of the initial evaluation and then the successful treatment for improving functioning. When clients come into a session as a couple, a family, or a group, they frequently have communication troubles. I often hear that a person does not know how to communicate or that they shut down when trying to talk or even that they do not take corrections well. The list goes on and on, but that information tells the counselor that there is a communication problem. It is imperative that an assessment is completed between the counselor and everyone in that system to determine the communication pattern. Sometimes, someone might demonstrate a healthy pattern of communication, but the person (or organization) they are attempting to interact with demonstrates a very unhealthy pattern of communication. Knowing the patterns of communication—both ours and others'—can open our eyes to understanding how to proceed. Across all patterns of communication exist certain behaviors that accompany variations of body language in interactions with others. The rest of this chapter will explore three unhealthy patterns of communication (passive, aggressive, and passive-aggressive) as well as the healthy pattern of assertive communication.

The first pattern of communication is commonly termed passive communication. When someone exhibits this pattern of communication, they are prioritizing the needs, wants, and feelings of others and not their own. This person does not express their own needs, especially when they are the opposite of what another person needs. They don't stand up for themselves, which often appears as being softer spoken and quiet, having poor eye contact (sometimes looking down when communicating), and exhibiting an overall lack of confidence. As a result of these behaviors, passive communicators are easily taken advantage of due to their people-pleasing nature and their inability to say no, causing misunderstandings with others as well. This type of communicator is commonly referred to as a "doormat." This is strong language, but it rings true. Other folks learn very quickly that they can step all over these types to get what they want. I often say that I am a survivor of my own passive communication patterns, so I can easily provide an example from my own life. I'd been working since the age of 15 and have been promoted to different positions. In each one I'd demonstrate effectiveness in one task, and thus it was not very long until I'd be asked to take on another. Unfortunately, I was always unable to say no, even though I was often overloaded and underpaid. In each job I did, I'd end up overworked, underpaid, overstressed, and unable to see that I was creating the problem. When I look back, I see that if I'd just said no, I could have avoided the overload. Of course, I know now that my passive communication pattern was directly linked back to my childhood with an NPD mother. Saying no was not an option, especially in my mother's world.

The communication pattern these passive communicators most fear is that of the aggressive communicator. You might be thinking about your NPD abuser, who is quite aggressive in their style of interacting with others. Aggressive communicators trumpet their own needs, wants, and feelings at the expense of other people's needs being met. The people in their path are commonly bullied and their needs ignored. Aggressive communicators are often driven by anger and hold a hostile stance against others, which creates a highly toxic environment. They find it very easy to stand up for their beliefs, but they are often unwilling to compromise; moreover, they criticize, humiliate, and dominate others through the use of loud and overbearing behavior. They frequently interrupt others, refuse to listen, are disrespectful, and boast an "in your face" stance while crossing others' boundaries verbally and/or physically. They can be scary—and for good reason. Imagine being a retail cashier and an aggressive person comes into your line; when you let the person know their item is not on sale, they unleash a barrage of filthy language on you. They attempt to control you by demanding a discount, raising their voice, and humiliating and bullying you. The aggressor does not stop until their goal is accomplished: a discount. You may be thinking this behavior is too ridiculous for a discount, but unfortunately, this type of behavior does scare people into compliance and/or lead to a law enforcement call.

Another type of significant communication pattern is the passive-aggressive communication pattern. This is often overlooked because people cannot fathom that a person could have this combination, but think of this more as an outward passivity with internal aggression. Individuals who are passive-aggressive communicators do not directly communicate their feelings, but those negative emotions lurk beneath the surface. Because those negative emotions are beneath the surface, these types express emotions such as anger and unhappiness in subtle and indirect ways. How does this look? Well, an individual might use sarcasm, indirect communication, avoidant conversation, or ghosting, and they are often considered "the ultimate saboteur." They may resort to eye rolling, hunched shoulders, and saying one thing but doing another, such as saying yes but meaning no. They may using words such as fine, whatever, and okay. When describing something, they may use phrases such as "per our past conversation," "for future reference," or even give you the silent treatment.

The passive-aggressive communicator can be quite difficult to deal with as well. In my work with communication, I have found that as individuals progress from being passive to more assertive, they tend to exhibit passive-aggressive styles of communication. It can feel a bit safer to avoid, ignore, or roll their eyes than to say what they desire. A good example of a passive-aggressive response would be as follows: imagine that you've pitched an idea at work, and your boss loves it, but a colleague is asked their perception of it. They respond, "Yes, it is fine." Or imagine you have been asked to take on another task, and you've told yourself that this time, you will say no, but instead you say, "Whatever, I can do it." However, your tone and body language reveal your aggravation. The boss might even come back and ask, "Are you sure?" But you passive-aggressively reiterate, "It's fine." The boss leaves a bit confused but figures that you gave your yes; meanwhile, you stew away, give the boss the silent treatment, and may not even complete the work.

The healthiest pattern of communication is assertive communication. Countless people confuse aggressive and assertive communication patterns, but they are very different. An assertive communicator considers the needs, wants, and feelings of themselves and others as well. When they interact, assertive communicators listen, do not interrupt, respect the other person(s), and validate what others are experiencing. The assertive communicator is confident, stands up for their own rights, and has a confident tone and open body language, along with good eye contact, possibly a smile, and a willingness to compromise. Additionally, an assertive communicator not only allows space for individuals to be honest but also promotes honesty, for they know it is necessary for growing and learning from each other. Individuals who are assertive are a breath of fresh air, as others express the relief it is to know what to expect from them and say these types have a calming presence. It is not difficult to see why this is the healthiest pattern. However, it takes practice to apply this style. Also, as I have noted in other chapters, some folks have enduring habits that make it challenging to adjust their communication pattern, especially due to lacking both insight and the desire to adjust. Now that we've journeyed together through these patterns of communication, please take some time to examine the example below, review the reactions based upon the communication pattern, and then write the response that resonates with you from Table 8.3.

Example:

A friend asked to change the dinner date that has been planned for a month, and you'd worked your schedule around it already.

It would be helpful for you to take a few minutes to outline a situation with your NPD abuser and then write out the scenario, your response, and your abuser's response. Then indicate what your typical pattern of communication is.

Table 8.3. Communication Responses

Passive	Umm, yeah, do you need me to call everyone and let them know the date needs to change?
Aggressive	No way! Why do you think you have the right to change the date? You are crazy if you think that is going to happen.
Passive-Aggressive	Whatever, but for future reference, we already had a date and time planned.
Assertive	I hate that you cannot be there, but I've had it on my calendar for a month, and so have the other folks. I am going to keep the scheduled date.

NPD abuser scenario:

_____

_____

_____

Your response:

_____

_____

_____

Type of communication pattern:

_____

_____

_____

NPD abuser response:

_____

_____

_____

Type of communication pattern:

_____

_____

_____

As you continue to read this chapter, please take a moment to really give yourself some self-compassion, and receive this virtual hug from me, as I know that all of this information is quite intense. Yet you have grown from it, so please take note of how you are changing through this process. You have learned a lot about yourself and your relationship dynamics so far and that there are always solutions available for improving your skills, especially with communication patterns. Relationships are impacted by communication but are influenced by other individuals, whether they are friends, family, colleagues, or even society as a whole. It is important to realize that, as it is with all change, the only person you can control is yourself—your thoughts, emotions, and behavioral responses. Now let's delve into how to be more assertive in your relationships.

Over time I have learned that to develop and maintain healthy relationships, it is important I show up as my authentic self, but I also need to remind myself that I teach others how to treat me through my interactions. By this I mean that by not saying no, by having loose boundaries, and/or by allowing folks to take advantage of my time, I have taught others what I will allow. It is critical that they know I will set clear boundaries and will compromise when it is appropriate but also that I will not be taken advantage of. As you have read so far, being assertive leads to behaviors that enable you to get your needs met while respecting the needs of others. Let's explore how you can learn to clearly state your needs and wants, as well as maintain boundaries. Let's begin with your body language. It is critically important to maintain good eye contact and an appropriate, steady tone of voice—not too low or too high. In 2012 Amy Cuddy encouraged TED Talk listeners to adopt a body posture like that of a superhero, which is also referred to as the superwoman/man pose. The movement emphasized considering your posture, as the pose sets a tone of confidence and elevates self-esteem; thus it is a good tool to use when you want to demonstrate confident body language, which aligns with assertiveness.

It may not be helpful to you if you're mimicking the way you imagine a superhero stands, but it is a great reminder to stand tall, with your chin up and body language open. Along with your body language, it is important to reflect on your self-talk.

Consider what you tell yourself regarding personal respect. Your needs and wants are just as valid as anyone else's. Just as you respect others, those within your circle should respect you as well. Part of respect involves an openness to your thoughts, feelings, and opinions. Of course, expressing your thoughts and emotions in a calm manner, a goal of becoming assertive, helps the other person stay calm and not escalate their response. And if they do escalate, when you remain calm, even when they push, you've learned to not allow them to get under your skin. To be confident in expressing yourself, whether with your NPD abuser or someone else, you need to practice. This means practicing what you're going to say when you want your desires, needs, and values met. Individuals have their own personal values, needs, and desires, which are not good or bad: they just are what they are. Consequently, it is okay to say no to others, as there is no way to make everyone happy. When you practice what you might say, you build confidence and get more comfortable with saying no or offering an alternative solution to the person.

Years ago, when I was working on becoming more assertive, I explored various ways to build those skills. I encountered many different perspectives that led me to recognize that it was more important to believe in my right to speak up for myself and to live according to my own needs than simply to practice skills. There were three primary skills I had to learn through practice. And I needed to practice with someone safe (looking in a mirror to practice the language also works). The first skill that I learned was the use of "I" statements. When you use the "I" statement, you take responsibility for your feelings without blaming the other person. This is particularly useful to use with NPD abusers who are very defensive. Although you cannot change their defensiveness, your use of "I" statements enables your own honest reflections. When using an "I" statement, consider this formula: "I feel *emotion word* when *explanation*." Some variations of "I feel" include "I am," "I need," or "I want." Let's shift from using the weighted word "you" in these conversations to using our "I" statements. It can take some practice, so let's review how phrases can be adjusted, using the following examples: "I feel hurt when you ignore me"; "I don't agree when plans are changed last minute"; "I am tired when we stay out so late"; or "I feel aggravated when I come home and the house is such a mess."

The second skill I learned offered ways to get out of bad situations, especially when backed into a corner (literally or figuratively). By the time you feel backed into a corner, the abuser has likely become very escalated. To defuse this, it is important to acknowledge the other person's emotions and provide another time to circle back to the conversation. This should be done with a balanced voice, without raising pitch or volume. For example,

"I hear your frustration. It's understandable to have this emotion. I would like to continue this conversation tomorrow, once we've had some sleep" or "I appreciate your point of view. It's natural that we will not agree on every topic. I would like for us to agree to disagree."

The final skill is the use of the "broken record." To the folks who do not know what a broken record is (how wonderful that there has been a recent resurgence of record players!), please read this explanation: when a record is on a turntable, if it is scratched, it will skip and then repeat the same verses of the song over and again. We can mimic the broken record in a helpful technique for assertive communication. The broken-record technique is a powerful skill to use when someone is trying to manipulate you, which is quite common with NPD abuse. To apply this skill, you will repeat the same phrase firmly and repeatedly. Sometimes, you use the exact same phrase, and other times, the phrase is stated in a slightly different way. For example, you may say, "I feel so hurt when you yell at me about my choices in friends." Then as the person continues to be aggressive, you reiterate, "I feel so hurt when you yell at me about my choices in friends." The other option, continuing the broken record but changing how it is said, could sound like this: "It makes me so hurt when you yell at me about my choices in friends" or "It is frustrating to listen to negative statements said about my friends." We may be apprehensive of using this technique for fear it will escalate the NPD abuser (or someone else who is aggressive). Remember that they will be aggressive no matter the tactic you use. So why not use the broken-record technique or one of the other assertiveness skills? Through my own use of these skills, I've found that the person sometimes gets angry with this technique, but then I can exit the bad situation when I add an "I" statement. Using one—or both—of them has always worked for me, so please do not hesitate to try these.

As I was working on my healing from NPD abuse, I was exposed to the use of emotion-focused therapy (EFT). As a counselor, I'd known about the theory, but I'd not used all the tenets associated with it. I had a counselor assist me with applying the skills from EFT, but I was left with a sense of missing something; I'd not gotten specific tools to help me with effective communication and healthy management of my relationships. When I became certified to take part in a dialectical behavioral therapy (DBT) treatment team and then certified as a dialectical behavioral therapist, I began to use the tools accompanying DBT practices for my own purposes, and a world of possibilities opened up to me. In this section, I explore a few skills from EFT and then delve into some of the interpersonal effectiveness strategies developed by Marsha Linehan as part of her skills protocol in DBT (Linehan, 2015).

EFT focuses on the importance that emotions have in influencing personal change. This theory seeks to assist individuals and couples with having an enhanced awareness of their emotions. With this awareness comes an eventual level of acceptance of how emotions influence one's relationships and lives, leading an individual to learn to express emotions effectively and in a healthy and regulated manner. Some of the primary tenets of EFT are empowering self, balance, and thus creating change and meaning in one's life (Greenberg, 2017). I am not an expert on EFT, but I do think it is critical for us to recognize that, as human beings, we have a range of emotions (e.g., anger, sadness, fear, frustration) and that we should validate our emotions but also learn how to manage them effectively.

As a teenager, I would tell my friends that I do not get angry. I truly believed that I did not get angry, and still, to this day, my anger outbursts are rare. Later in life, I realized that I'd stifled my anger due to my life experiences. I was not allowed room for anger, so I often believed it was not a good emotion, as it could cause harm to others. Instead of this approach, I needed to be taught how our emotional system is a necessary motivational system we need throughout life and that it should be explored and expressed (Greenberg, 2017). What I learned from my EFT therapist is to get out of my head and into my emotions, as well as to be okay with whatever emotion should emerge. She taught me that "sucking it up," as I was often told to do as a child, would not help me. I have long been the queen of analyzing situations and stuffing emotions, so I had to learn that whenever something would happen, I should sit in the initial emotional response, staying with that emotion, then reflect and journal about it—this versus going straight into my thoughts.

As I delved more into EFT while researching for this book, I found that it offers many other strategies that would have been useful to me, including the use of de-escalation, which now assists me with stepping outside of stressful situations to observe the emerging behaviors and emotions. Additionally, via this method, I've learned how to restructure the varied perspectives regarding behaviors and emotions. In other words, EFT has helped me get beneath the surface of why these negative interactions unfold. Finally, I've learned how to integrate new solutions to the problems, and thus, a new awareness of emotions has emerged from the new solution (Greenberg, 2017). This brief overview of EFT does not do it justice, but this simple framework should explain why I've used it some. Remember that in order to survive the NPD relationship, I always had to see the problem, behavior, or emotions from my abuser's perspective, with little room for my own thoughts and emotional responses. It is still hard for me to avoid going into my thoughts and to allow my emotions to emerge. Though it remains a challenge, I am much better than I was. I encourage you to consider investigating EFT further or even to try the simple technique I was taught.

Now, let's examine some of the powerful tools provided in Marsha Linehan's work (under her skills modules specific to interpersonal effectiveness; Linehan, 2015). I consider her research and work a catalyst to major changes in my interactions with people and relationships, as it taught me valuable skills. There was a clear focus in her work on learning how to effectively get what we want from another person, on how to maintain, improve, or disconnect from unhealthy relationships while also maintaining one's self-respect.

If you have a healthy relationship in your life where you can effectively get what you want from another individual, but you'd like to improve engagement, try the DEARMAN technique. As you go through the steps of each letter, first consider how you can apply it to someone you deem as safe, then consider if it would be effective with your NPD abuser. The examples I provide are based upon examples of a situation with a potential NPD abuser.

DEARMAN Technique

(Adapted from Linehan, 2015)

D: Describe the situation. It is important to evaluate the situation that has unfolded based upon the facts and not opinions.
Example: "You texted me and said to meet at the restaurant at 6:00 p.m., and it is now 8:00 p.m."

E: Express your feelings about the situation because no one can read your mind and automatically know how you feel about something. This is where the "I" statements we practiced earlier really come in handy.
Example: "When you say you will arrive at 6:00 p.m. and you arrive at 8:00 p.m. instead, I get frustrated."

A: Assert yourself by asking for what you want or say no very clearly. Make the request very specific.
Example: "I would like you to notify me if you will be later than 15 minutes."

R: Reinforce what you are hoping will happen ahead of time. As you think of this one, you may feel it is similar to how we have learned to outmanipulate the manipulator. However, this technique considers what you will get out of it *as well as* what the other person will, so it is fair in a way manipulation is not.

Example: "I would be so grateful to know you are going to be a few minutes late. I will do the same for you if I know I am going to be late."

M: Be mindful of your ultimate goal. Maintain your focus on what you want while remaining calm. Do you want to be heard and understood? Do not allow the other person to distract you from your position, get you off topic, or change your mind due to their level of verbal attack.

This is an important time to use the broken-record technique I mentioned earlier: say the same thing over and over again. Do not respond to personal attacks, and keep to your point.

Example: "I would rather you notify me if you will be later than 15 minutes. I would rather you notify me if you will be later than 15 minutes."

A: Appear confident by using an effective tone of voice, good eye contact, and a balanced facial expression. Stay away from saying things such as "I am sorry" or "I am not sure" or using a lower voice, such as a whisper, or looking down. Remember the superhero pose we discussed earlier with assertiveness skills.

N: Negotiation is important, but it cannot be a 100% compromise, with only you negotiating. Ask yourself what you are willing to compromise or to consider. Sometimes, with an NPD abuser, they will not negotiate if they know you'll bend at least a little, so consider asking them what solution they would consider if they were in the same situation. If it is not reasonable, stick to your same phrase.

Example: "What can we do about this? . . . I am not willing to wait 2 hours at a restaurant."

Now that you have practiced a technique to assist with improving your relationships by getting what you want, let's look at a way to effectively maintain a relationship in a healthy manner. Validation is not something we are accustomed to from our NPD abusers. In fact, we might have been so invalidated over time that we do not think we deserve to be validated. Sometimes, the practice of validating others can help us learn the importance of self-validation, which we discussed earlier in this book. A key element of DBT is the use of validation (Linehan, 2015). Although Linehan did not come up with the following acronym, I think it is useful to apply validation in our lives.

ACT Technique

A: Acknowledge that a person's thoughts, emotions, and behaviors have causes and could be understandable in a given situation. This does not mean agreeing with the person or giving them pity, but it allows space for there to be a kernel of truth in the other's stance.
Situation: You and your kids went out to eat without your partner and did not think to tell the person.
Response: "I can understand how you would be upset because we did not ask you to come eat out with us."

C: Closeness is what individuals desire within relationships. Thus, validating another's perspective reduces the pressure to prove who is right and who is wrong, reduces unhealthy emotions, and makes problem-solving possible. As you already know, invalidation is painful.

T: Taking a stance to validate an element of someone's perspective and situation reinforces the importance that all individuals, including yourself, deserve validation. Remember that validation does not mean you condone a behavior or situation; it means you can see the perspective of another person. We should be willing to offer to others what we desire for ourselves.

The final area that was addressed by Linehan in her work on interpersonal effectiveness is the importance of knowing how to end destructive relationships (Linehan, 2015). While in an NPD abusive relationship, you likely thought about this many times. You might be asking yourself, How do I get out? Or if you have already exited the relationship, your question shifts: How do I avoid unhealthy relationships? This is less of a technique to apply in your life and more of a mindset to consider. The first thing that you need to understand is the difference between a destructive and an interfering relationship. A destructive relationship ruins the quality of the relationship the other person and with yourself. They might start out fine but, over time, become destructive, threatening your safety with physical violence and degradation of your self-esteem, causing you unhappiness and impacting your sense of peace. Contrastingly, an interfering relationship is one that gets in the way of your pursuit of goals, hobbies, and other relationships in your life. These might impact your friends, family, work, and other pursuits (Linehan, 2015).

Here is a note of caution: please stop for a minute and ask yourself if you are currently or have been previously in a destructive or in an interfering relationship. This is a serious consideration, as it can mean the difference in how your life functions. Domestic violence, now considered interpersonal violence, is defined as any relationship that threatens your physical well-being. If this applies to you, please seek out help from law enforcement and your local interpersonal-violence resources. These are not relationships that can be improved via the use of assertiveness skills, DEARMAN, or ACT. We have to know when to ask for help, and if you are in a violent relationship, it is the time to seek out help. For interfering relationships, you have more power. You can implement assertiveness skills, DEARMAN, and ACT, as well as ask a clinical professional to help supplement the skills that you are using.

This chapter has provided a comprehensive overview of the impact of relationships. We interact in this world with other people, so it is natural that we will have some problems with communication in our interactions. We can learn to improve some of these problems, especially regarding communication patterns, while others might need to be severed for our own physical and mental well-being. I encourage you to stop for a minute and do a quick review of this chapter; make a note of one area you really need to practice. Before you move to the next chapter, I encourage you to take some time to journal and reflect upon the relationships in your life and what goals you need to set for yourself.

CHAPTER 9

~

Understanding and Managing Emotions

All human beings have the capacity for feeling and experiencing emotions. Emotions are an individual's conscious mental reactions based their subjective experience—let's break that down a bit. Emotions do not happen without our awareness. Yes, the emotions might come pouring out, but we are consciously aware of them as they flow. How do I know this? Scientific research has been carried out to explain this phenomenon, but to gain a practical understanding, consider that: when an emotion arises, we often say things like "I do not know why I am acting this way" or "I have a right to feel this way." Humans typically either want to express or suppress. There are some individuals who use emotions as a weapon, like our NPD abusers. They often express their emotions about a specific object or event, which can include an actual physical experience or situation or even a connection to other human beings.

Emotions lead to physiological and behavioral changes in our body. Consider the anger you've felt in your life. You become aware of your thoughts racing, your body temperature adjusting, and the feeling of clenched teeth, and then the behavioral response comes. How long the emotional response lasts varies based on the individual's personality and genetics, as well as how they implement specific skills for lowering levels of arousal. As I've spoken about in other chapters, many survivors of NPD abuse do not give themselves permission to feel emotions and will often stuff them, pretend they are not having them, or not understand the range of emotions pouring out.

Chapter 9 focuses on the importance of acknowledging and learning how to express emotions in an effective manner. When we are in the clutches of NPD abuse, our emotions can be hard to recognize and effectively regulate. You have likely been taught to not trust your emotions, or you believe you must deprive yourself of varied emotional responses to please the NPD abuser. Yet it is imperative to know them, understand them, and learn how to express, monitor, and master them. This chapter explores the array of emotions, their purpose, their expression, and how to regulate them.

Understanding Emotions and Behavioral Responses

As I stated in the introduction, emotions are a necessary part of life. I am an animal lover, and it hurts me when individuals say that animals do not have emotions, especially because humans are animals, and we have emotions. I often can see emotions in my own pets. I think it is important to validate the emotions that we and others are experiencing (even animals). It is important to understand that there is a purpose in having emotions. We need them because they are messages that signal that some large internal or external event is unfolding in our lives. I think about the emotional reaction I had to a very bad leg injury or the emotions that emerged when I had my children. In the one example, tears of pain brought a physiological release to the physical affliction of my leg injury; in the other, tears of joy, happiness, and wonder followed the birth of a child. There is the same reality—having tears—but they are due to different experiences. The experiences and emotions vary from person to person. So the first thing to realize about emotions is that they are necessary but oftentimes unclear, especially as humans experience vast ranges of emotions. As a result, we will stop here to delve into a few emotions that humans experience, which are outlined in Table 9.1.

Now that you have reviewed several of the emotions, the words associated with these emotions, how these emotions might be expressed, and the consequences relating to them, consider what you might want to add to this list. This chart in no way encompasses all the emotions you have experienced, but it is important to note the primary emotion listed along with its associated words. The associated words are also other emotion words, and you likely recognize many of them but might not know what they feel like within your body. It is important to acknowledge those you do recognize. You likely recognize some of these emotions from the times they were directed right at you by your NPD abuser. Your NPD abuser trained you to think it was okay for them to exhibit their emotions, but you were not "allowed" to feel or express them. You learned to stuff them rather than express them outwardly. It is time to no longer stuff your emotions but to learn to express them.

Table 9.1. Emotions

Emotion	Words Associated With the Emotion	Expression of Emotion	Consequence of Emotion
Anger	Bitter, furious, irritated, rage, annoyed, irritated, outrage, vengeful	Physically or verbally attacking, frowning or have a mean expression, body tightening up, hands clenching, red or flushed face, sarcasm, crying	• Pushing others away • Scaring others • Unhealthy thinking patterns • Loss of job, partner, or friend • Getting one's point across • Protection of self
Sadness	Sorrow, hurt, alone, depressed, suffering, gloomy, disappointed, insecure, melancholy, woeful	Avoidance, helplessness, withdrawn, moping, brooding, talking very little, frowning, slumped posture, head down, crying, loss of pleasure	• Not being able to see the good in the world • Thoughts are flooded about sad things • Irritable, self-blame or others-oriented blame, poor sleeping and appetite
Disgust	Dislike, aversion, disdain, loathing, hate, repelled, repulsed, vile, sickened, repugnant, aversion	Vomiting, looking away, avoiding food or drink, pushing or kicking away, cursing, frowning, grimacing, smirking, sarcastic tone, being disrespectful	• Leaving a situation • Thoughts consumed with what was observed or experienced, hyperawareness of object of disgust
Fear	Anxiety, dread, worry, terror, shock, on edge, horror, nervous, apprehension, uneasy	Fleeing, running, walking briskly, hiding from or avoiding, trembling voice, sweaty, heart racing, crying, screaming, asking for help	• Fleeing a harmful situation • Being hypervigilant when there is no threat, losing control, more avoidance, thoughts are consumed with past or future threats
Happiness	Joy, relief, jolly, cheerful, excitement, elation, pleasure, ecstasy, bliss, relief, enjoyment, optimism, pride, glee, pleasure	Smiling, laughing, silliness, saying positive and uplifting words and actions, hugging, jumping up and down, being talkative and expressing excitement	Doing nice things for others, expression of friendliness, positive perspective about self and others, seeing the good in others, less worry and more expectation of future happy times

(continued)

Table 9.1. Emotions (Continued)

Emotion	Words Associated With the Emotion	Expression of Emotion	Consequence of Emotion
Guilt	Culpability, remorse, apologetic, regret, sorry	Trying to repair the harm, make amends for the wrongdoing, fix the damage, ask for forgiveness, apologizing, confessing, giving gifts	• Making resolutions to change • Making changes in behavior • Potential for developing a sense of shame • Not being able to release the guilt
Jealousy	Watchful, defensive, cautious, clingy, fear of losing someone or something, clutching, defensive, suspicious, rivalrous	Attempting to control the freedom of another due to fear of losing the person, accusatory language or expression of disloyalty, spying on others, interrogating others about their behaviors and choices, dependency, increased or excessive demonstrations of love	• Seeing the worst in others, losing the person or making the person fearful; thoughts are preoccupied with suspicion • Narrow mind and focus on object of jealousy

I purposefully added the emotion of guilt on the feelings chart, for I've heard survivors talk about their guilt far too often. It was mentioned so much that I started spending time intentionally breaking down the behaviors of the survivor, asking them about guilt being the strongest emotion they felt, especially when they'd rarely, if ever, committed an egregious act. Oftentimes, the NPD abuser had twisted and manipulated the situation so much that these survivors felt as if they had caused harm in some way, and thus, the guilt emerged. We explore unwarranted emotions like guilt later in this chapter.

For now, I would like you to take a few minutes to write down a few experiences you've had in your life; outline the strongest emotion and then your subsequent behavioral response in Table 9.2. I first write an example as a guide for you, and then you can move forward with your own work. Following Table 9.2, I provide a rationale for this. Remember that the situation may be good, bad, or even neutral, but we all tend to remember both the most difficult and the most wonderful experiences. For the purposes of this text, I chose to share an example that would be considered more disappointing.

Table 9.2. Emotional Experiences

Experience	Strongest Emotion	Behavioral Response
Example: I received a call from a potential employer who said that I did not get a job at the university, and I'd felt certain I would.	Sadness, hurt, disappointment	I verbally complained how I felt I deserved the opportunity. I blamed the university.

So what is the rationale for this activity? The purpose is to highlight how our experiences and emotions are linked. When something happens, we get an initial emotional and physiological response, while within an abusive relationship, it is very likely that your body physiologically responds before you have time to think and recognize your emotions. It is after the assault ends, whether physical or verbal, that the emotions might start flooding in. Then comes the behavioral response, determined by this emotion. Within an NPD abusive relationship, the behavioral response is typically aligned with self-preservation, along with an attempt to avoid escalating the abuser. Thus, the survivor often learns to stifle their emotions and subsequent behaviors. The first time the abuser scares the survivor, the survivor may experience a strong verbal or emotional reaction. But over time, due to the NPD abuser's counter to their reaction, the survivor learns their emotional and behavioral response is not safe, so they adapt them to please the person and avoid the abusive reaction.

As time advances, you become so good at reading your abuser's emotions and subsequent reaction(s) that you can tell the best way to respond with just a glance from that person. You can see how understanding your emotions in a relationship is connected to your experiences. So go back and review your experiences, and if you have not added in an experience related to your NPD abuser, please consider doing so now. Write that experience down in Table 9.2, and add your strongest emotion and your behavioral response from that time. Pause, take a deep breath, and ask yourself, What would be your preferred behavioral response? Outline your response in Table 9.3.

You have the right to feel your emotions and respond in a way that does not harm you or anyone else. You should not have to stifle your emotions.

Table 9.3. Preferred Behavioral Response

Experience	Strongest Emotion	Behavioral Response as a Survival Tactic	Preferred Behavioral Response

We all have emotions, but it is essential to acknowledge how some emotions can be harmful to us when we consistently experience them. This takes us back to the feeling of guilt. I spent most of my adolescence and early adulthood feeling guilty. I would feel guilty when I perceived I'd hurt someone's feelings, I felt I'd disappointed my parents, or I'd thought something awful about someone, and sometimes I'd replay conversations or events to determine if I'd said or done something wrong. I now realize I should not have experienced that guilt. Why? I'd done nothing wrong. I did not lie, steal, cheat, scream, hurt someone's feelings, or do some horrible act to another. Of course, if I do hurt someone's feelings today, I feel guilty and will apologize. However, due to my NPD exposure, I was put in a position, especially as the scapegoat of my family, where guilt was layered on me. I knew I had to get out from under all the self-blame because feeling it so much led me to constant apologizing, with me saying, "I am sorry." When I was in my early thirties, a dear friend of mine, who is now deceased, looked at me and said, "Stop saying you are sorry. You have not done anything wrong." For some reason her words hit me, and I made it my goal that year to stop saying sorry unless I'd truly done something that warranted an apology. It is important that we check the facts of a situation to determine if they are congruent with the emotions we are experiencing. This approach of tackling thinking patterns is drawn from cognitive behavioral therapy and rational emotive behavioral therapy, which I have been using in counseling pratice for over 20 years. However, we must take the next step and ask additional questions to determine if our emotions fit our situations. To understand the importance of checking the facts, we need to reflect a bit on how we as human beings can use our thoughts to analyze when and how something is happening. When I asked you to evaluate your emotions earlier, I specifically asked you to outline an experience, your strongest emotion, and then your behavioral response. I purposely did not want you to get too caught up in evaluating your thoughts. If I'd asked about those first, you might have focused only on them and been stuck in your head. It is important to understand that we are first emotional and then thinking beings who have the right to emote as well as analyze. Beck (cognitive behavioral therapy [CBT]; 1976), Ellis (rational emotive behavioral therapy [REBT]; 2023), and Linehan (dialectical behavior therapy [DBT]; 2015) all published their theories highlighting how we humans often believe we have an automatic, uncontrollable response to the things that happen to us. Realistically, we might have an automatic physiological response, but our thoughts influence our emotions and thus our subsequent behaviors. For a bit more clarity, see the image in Figure 9.1, which shows the impact of thoughts on emotions.

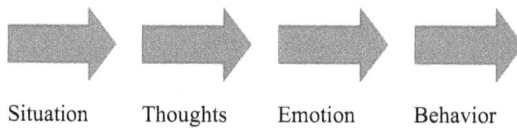

Situation   Thoughts   Emotion   Behavior

Figure 9.1. Linking Thoughts, Emotions, and Behavior

These theories—CBT, REBT, and DBT—are supported by numerous studies and have been used by clients with different symptoms. As an NPD survivor, you likely have some of these symptoms, such as anxiety, sadness, worry, and maybe even a clinical diagnosis of depression. I have used these methods for clients struggling with dysfunctional relationships, including ones affected by interpersonal violence, depression, anxiety, and/or even a personality disorder. These theories emphasize helping clients recognize the thoughts that lead to their unhealthy emotions. When something happens, we often have an immediate reaction, called automatic thoughts. That explains the ubiquitous belief that we have an emotion because something happened to us. For example, let's say you got dressed up to head out to a party, and you asked your partner how you looked. If that person were to respond, "It is not the best color on you," you'd have an emotional reaction like sadness or even anger, which would then influence your behavior—that is, changing clothes. CBT and REBT explain that an emotional reaction is due to an automatic thought or self-talk that can be distorted. So it is not what the person said that made you have an emotional reaction but what you thought about what was said to you. This can be a challenging to acknowledge, but it's important to understand that not all individuals would feel an unhealthy emotion. In fact, there could be a variety of emotional reactions to that same situation. One might respond and say, "Well, I love this color, I look great and feel good!" Someone else might say, "Oh no, what should

I wear then? I did not know it looked so bad." This plethora of differing emotional reactions influences what behavior will follow.

Realistically, it can take us some time to recognize the impact of our thoughts on our emotions and behaviors. Also, the focus on how thoughts influence emotions may not resonate with everyone. This is okay—I want to remind you that you have autonomy and can make the decisions that are best for you. That is the purpose of this book: to help you not only heal but also grow. Sometimes, the behavior change might need to occur first, and then the thoughts will adjust. I have tried this in my life. Sometimes, my thoughts have kept me stuck in a cycle. So getting out of my head and into the present often takes a behavior shift. I would activate the new behavior by changing my routine, doing the opposite action, as is discussed later in this chapter, a behavioral replacement, such as swapping a frown for a smile.

When you find a thought emerging about a situation, you are having an automatic thought. That thought influences your emotions. I would like you to return to the emotion of guilt. Imagine that you get a lunch break and decide to go to the local park that is 5 minutes away. You sit on a blanket out in the sunshine and eat your picnic lunch. It is so warm outside and you become so relaxed that you doze off. You wake up later than expected and look at your watch, realizing you only have 2 minutes to get back to work. Immediately, your thoughts start racing as you think, "I am going to get in trouble," "They are going to fire me," or "I am such an idiot!" With these thoughts flowing, guilt may easily follow. Once this guilt comes upon you, you face a decision regarding your next action. What comes next? Possibly an apology? However, when you arrive, other coworkers returning from their lunch break are walking in at the same time as you. They are not apologizing for being late, but you feel so guilty, you plan to apologize anyway. But why would you apologize if they are not? The boss does not seem bothered by the 2-minute tardiness. The guilt you feel is way too intense for this situation and would be considered an unhealthy emotion, given its surrounding climate. Thus, it is important we work on adjusting our thoughts so the emotions and subsequent behavior change. However, please note that it is critically important to check the facts of the situation and not exaggerate. You want to acknowledge your emotions and, at the same time, not merely react based on your perception that everyone within your circle (e.g., coworkers, friends, and other family members) will react the same way as your abuser. You have likely been, like I was, very conditioned to apologize, feel guilt, and have a behavioral response of self-blame. However, sometimes it is important to regulate your emotions by checking the facts, monitoring your thoughts about the situation, and sitting in the emotion (versus pushing it away), and sometimes we might need to adapt not only our thoughts that are linked to our emotions but also our behavior.

Why Talk About Emotions?

Now that you are aware that emotions are normal and that you will have them, it is critical to remember that we have emotions for a reason. Have you ever thought of it that way? You are likely wondering why we just talked about checking the facts that influence our emotions. Well, there is a balance: there comes a time when we need to consider adapting the emotion we are experiencing because it is causing more harm than necessary. However, sometimes, part of checking those facts includes acknowledging that the emotion you are feeling is valid for the circumstance. Sometimes, the emotion fits the situation. Think about watching a sad movie; meeting a child or grandchild, which brings you to tears; hearing that you got a promotion at work that you've been wanting; hearing how your child or friend was bullied; or hearing a song that reminds you of a loved one who has passed away. There may be a range of emotional responses that emerge. It is natural to want to alleviate emotional or physical pain when we are feeling some form of it. However, there are times when we need to sit in that emotional pain. We often assign a value to our emotions based upon thinking patterns, some of which we discussed earlier. From where do these thinking patterns emerge? They developed from our experiences. Ask yourself, what was I told about emotions? How were emotions demonstrated to me? Take a moment to review the list of emotions provided earlier in this chapter, and consider what emotions were demonstrated. I provided a few blank lines for you to write about a person in your life and their typical emotional response. An example to ponder come from a male client who indicated that he was not sure how to be sad, as he was always told, "Boys don't cry. Suck it up." This individual learned as a child to literally not feel or express sadness as an emotion.

Our experiences influence what thoughts we hold about specific emotions, which is where thinking patterns can become a problem. Yes, thoughts influence emotions, but sometimes, our thoughts can be so warped by our experiences that we will not express a normal emotion. Imagine being told that you've been laid off from a job you've had for 25 years, and it's not only the work you enjoy, but your coworkers seem like family to you. A natural reaction might be feeling anger or even sadness. If you try to stuff it, avoid it, or hide the reaction, that emotion will come out in some way. Consider, for a moment, allowing the emotion to flood you, not unlike a bucket of water being poured on your head. You feel that water, whether cold or hot, flow down your head, your ears, over your eyes, and all the way down to your toes. You cannot avoid it, but you know it will be over soon. Picture an emotion doing the same thing. Imagine that you saved up for a year and just bought a brand-new car, paid for with a substantial down payment. You are leaving work and driving in heavy traffic. Someone runs a stop sign and hits you on the passenger side. You are physically okay, but the front of your car is crushed. Allow whatever emotion emerges to well up. Consider where you feel it in your body, and let it span up and down, side to side, filling the space of your body and allowing the emotion to emerge. Remember, the emotion will not last forever.

Emotions are our voice. If you've avoided a particular emotion for so long you've lost the capacity to express it, be comforted: there are now ways to expose yourself to the emotion. Exposure therapy is a powerful method because it helps people face the very thing they are avoiding, but instead of doing it immediately, they are slowly exposed. For example, let's say I fear spiders. I would not start off by touching a spider; I would begin by talking about spiders, then work up to looking at a picture of a spider, then walking up to one, and so forth. It is a slow process. Challenging yourself to experience an emotion can begin with 10 seconds of allowing the emotion to come, which can then progress to 20 seconds. This eventually can grow to several minutes. You will begin to recognize that it is okay to feel the emotion and can then let it go and move on. The emotion will not last forever, just like the cold feeling of water being poured over your head eventually ends.

Fear of Overreacting

Earlier I explored guilt as a near-universal feeling that plagues NPD abuse survivors. Another emotion that has been quite evident is fear. This is not a "typical" fear, like the fear being in a dark alley or of an airplane suddenly dropping in the sky; this is a fear of overreacting emotionally and triggering the overreaction of the NPD abuser. This may be an especially true fear where there was not only emotional abuse but also physical abuse. Remember that you can always get support—you are not alone. However, sometimes, the fear, although grounded in your experience, may need to be challenged, especially when the emotions are valid for the given situation but you know your response will not lead to physical violence. Growing your voice and identity so you can heal first involves the decision to adjust your

Table 9.4. Typical and Opposite Reaction

Emotion	Typical Action	New Opposite Action
Fear	Avoidance	Approach her and walk straight into her office.

behavior. To accomplish this, consider how you would typically respond, then make a choice to respond in the opposite way. Linehan (2015) explored understanding what the opposite action is and defined it to help individuals understand its importance; she defined opposite action as "acting opposite to an emotion's action urge" (Linehan, 2015, p. 230). When you do this, the emotion can shift due to the change in your behavior. To understand this further, consider the following example from my story, which may also be typical of a response you've had to your narcissistic abuser. This occurred with a former supervisor of mine; I was so afraid she would call me into her office. I had this fear because she was very belittling and unkind. My typical reaction or urge was to avoid her all day—or at least as long as I could. My opposite action (and what I consequently needed to do) would have been to approach her, listen to her, and speak up if she were to belittle me. Please take a moment to pick a situation and/or person, and consider your typical reaction to them. Then consider what you would prefer to do instead, using Table 9.4.

Just as we explored the importance of exposing ourselves to uncomfortable emotions, it is important to slowly expose ourselves to new actions/behaviors. The more we do a behavior, the more it becomes a part of who we are and our natural reaction. I have personally improved so much in the avoidance arena, so when I now find myself wanting to avoid, I stop myself and face whatever that is. And typically, the outcome is far better than my thoughts could have imagined. I know that encounters do not always unfold as we'd hope, but this gives us the chance to not only engage an opposite behavior to what we'd typically do but also to practice assertiveness.

How Are You Defined?

It is frustrating to think that we are labeled as anything, especially when we hear the word "victim" when we'd prefer to use "survivor." I know it can be quite hard to read through these chapters and realize how much work you have to do because of someone else's behavior. It can seem unfair and frustrating, and it may even bring you moments of anger and sadness. I want you to feel those emotions. I understand these emotions, as I have felt them as well. And it would be great if the NPD abuser could just gain insight into their behaviors and make their own changes. Then maybe we, the survivors, would not have to do all the work. I am sure you have been gaslit, manipulated, and possibly slandered. As a result, individuals have often defined you based upon your NPD abuser's words. I am here to remind you that that their narrative is not your narrative. You have the power to determine the ending to your story and forge your own identity. I have worked with many clients over the years who struggle to find themselves, and I think it is imperative they consider their own definition of self. We have explored this before, but I want you to now add the realization that you have the right to your emotions, and this adds another layer to your newly emerging self. As you reflect, please consider these rights as an NPD abuse survivor, which I developed as a reminder that we can live beyond the messages we received from our narcissistic abusers and be our authentic selves.

Rights as an NPD Abuse Survivor

1. You have the right to make decisions that impact your life.
2. You have the right to say, "No."
3. You have the right to protest if you are being treated unfairly.
4. You have the right to your own thoughts and emotions.
5. You have the right to your own beliefs, values, and goals.
6. You have the right to set boundaries.
7. You have the right to change your mind.
8. You have the right to decide who is in your life and who is not.
9. You have a right to education, employment, and financial security.
10. You have the right to be your authentic self both externally and internally.
11. You have the right to do the work needed to heal.
12. You have the right to take back your power.

Thank you for hanging in with me as we've explored emotions from various angles throughout this chapter. I challenge you to recognize the span of emotions you have, as well as to learn which ones you need to learn how to embrace and those that you need to adjust to be more emotionally regulated. It is also critical to understand that no one has the right to keep us stuck in the same behavior(s) we've exhibited before—we have a right to change our minds and behaviors. That is why we can make the choice to do an opposite action to what is expected and to adjust our narrative anytime we would like.

CHAPTER 10

~

Learning How to Manage Heartache

I know you may want to skip over a chapter that lingers over the topic of heartache, but please stay with me. All of us know the pain of heartache in our lives—that gut-wrenching feeling of being unloved, lonely, lied about, and never quite good enough. Heartache can come in many forms, and I am sure you've had some experiences across your life that came to your mind when you saw this chapter title. We cannot measure heartache based on our own experiences, because the experience of heartache varies across individuals. What may be difficult for me, literally making my heart feel as if it were breaking, may not impact you in the same way. Let's take a minute to define heartache. It is emotional pain, a form of distress, that is sometimes characterized as sorrow, grief, and anguish. When attempting to define it, we find there are not many words to help fully explain it, so individuals are often left searching for words that could be adequate. Many of my clients who've experienced heartache typically say that it is very difficult to explain to others, but common descriptors they've shared include phrases such as a stabbing in the heart, gut-wrenching grief, and persistent sorrow.

You may be surprised, as was I, to hear that there is a diagnosis called broken-heart syndrome. I was made aware of it by a colleague who was diagnosed with it after having suffered a cardiac event. They told her it was linked to the multiple stressors in her life. "Takotsubo syndrome (TTS), also known as Takotsubo cardiomyopathy, broken-heart syndrome, or stress cardiomyopathy, is defined as a transient, reversible cardiac event that mimics an acute coronary syndrome" (Casagrande et al., 2021, p. 1). Increasing amounts of research studies are being published that support the link between life events, their psychological impact, and broken-heart syndrome (Forte et al., 2019; Thayer et al., 2012), thus highlighting how important it is to learn how to handle our stress levels in our lives, particularly when events cause us emotional distress. I cannot fully explain all of the science behind this syndrome or detail how many stressful events in one's life it would take to cause to it, but it reminds us that we need ways to cope with the wide variety of stressors that we encounter.

The importance of understanding how we need to heal from heartache is now evident. Exposure to NPD abuse is likely only one of many life events to have impacted you, and within that relationship alone, you likely endured multiple traumas that made you familiar with the feeling of being stabbed in the heart. I've had many of those experiences as well. Consider the following story from my experience: I'd received a call from my mother during a busy workday while on a 10-minute break between seeing clients at my private practice office.

> I picked up my cell phone to Mom yelling that Dad had gone outside the house with a gun, saying he was going to kill himself because of me. I immediately panicked and told Mom to call the police and to go help Dad. She continued to tell me that I'd made him suicidal—that it was all my fault. I told her to take the phone to Dad so I could talk with him. When she refused, I hung up on her and called Dad. Typically, he never answered, but he did this time. He answered the phone calmly, and in a panicked voice, I immediately asked, "Where are you? How are you?" He responded with confusion, saying he was at work. I told him exactly what Mom had told me. I could tell he did not quite know what to say, as she had not coached him and he'd not been expecting my call. He did say that he had been depressed but not suicidal, and then quickly added that I needed to make sure to call my mother more often. He said, "You know how Mom is."

Wow! No apology. No acknowledgment that Mom had done wrong as I spoke with my father, sobbing. Then add to that horror that she'd said I was to blame for his suicidal behavior. That ripped my heart out and tore it into little pieces—and this was just one incident. I've had far too many of these types of stressful events cause distress and heartache. There is no way to convey to others the level of pain these types of mind games inflict on a person's psyche and the lasting effects.

So far, we have explored the varied skills necessary to foster the healing process and, specifically, the importance of understanding and managing emotions. Then we've acknowledged how experiences influence one's heartache. This heartache is easily perpetuated by the cycles that occur within NPD abusive relationships. These cycles of violence are similar to those where power and control tactics are used. Understanding these cycles provides us insight, but we additionally need to learn how to manage the distress that unfolds due to these cycles.

There are many words for describing the way an NPD abuser engages with others: they use drama, violence, and power and control, or a manipulation cycle. After earning my master's degree, I landed my first job in a domestic violence shelter. I remember my training on what was called the power and control wheel and the cycle of violence. The power and control wheel, drawn from what was termed as the Duluth model (Pence & Paymer, 1993), is relevant to the work of individuals within and outside of the NPD abusive relationship. This model examines the impact that power and control have in any relationship and across varied domains. Of course, when this model was originally developed, it was focused more on men as the abusers, with women receiving the abuse, in a typical domestic relationship. This is not as applicable in the research today, which exposes varied types of interpersonal relationships and dynamics within intimate and acquaintance relationships. Many of the elements noted by the Duluth model (Pence & Paymar, 1993) also perpetuate the cycles within an abusive NPD relationship.

As I explore each of these components of power and control in this next paragraph, ask yourself how these apply to your NPD relationship. It is common for narcissists to intimidate through their varied looks, actions, and gestures toward you or others. Emotional abuse includes tactics like calling you names, putting you down, calling you crazy, humiliating you, and making you feel guilty as if you have done something wrong. Also, they consistently minimize, deny their wrongdoing, and blame you for any problems that have unfolded. Isolating you from others, as well as hobbies or interests, as a way they commonly maintain control, along with financial control and coercion (Pence & Paymar, 1993). As I reflected on my own history with NPD exposure, I saw all these behaviors used in various ways. They ranged from being required to purchase the invitations for my own high school graduation to putting stipulations on any plans I had, whether it was to get a job in high school or my plans for college. There was so much coercion and emotional abuse, then denial of it when confronted about the behavior. Then add to this the following reality: when this type of power and control is perpetuated, the continued cycle of violence is very difficult to pull away from, as it's all an individual is accustomed to.

Walker (1989) researched what she proposed as the cycle of violence to help the public understand violent relationships and how that cycle can perpetuate in families, keeping individuals trapped within. Some of the elements are clearly very similar to the cycles perpetuated by an NPD abuser, but I would argue some are not. Walker (1979) explained how the typical cycle of abuse starts with the victim's attunement to the feeling of heightened tension rising. It is that sense that there is something in the air, a buildup of negative energy, that they cannot quite pinpoint at that moment. It might come from the look of the abuser, their body language, or even their tone of voice. Then, sometimes without warning, an incident occurs: the abuser lashes out physically, verbally, psychologically, or sexually. The behavior is clearly directed at the victim, and it can cause varying levels of pain, but the worst is the psychological harm. Next comes the reconciliation, where the abuser will make excuses for the behavior, often blaming the victim, and they may even resort to gaslighting. This is typically when an apology happens, but with an NPD abuser, they rarely apologize, which is where the cycle might differ; but there is clear gaslighting and blaming. If a narcissist does indeed apologize, it becomes a tool of manipulation to get you to move past the incident. Finally, there is a sense of calm, which can last for a while and feels good, and you can almost feel that all will be okay. Unfortunately, the cycle will continue with the tension building, an incident occurring, and reconciliation and calm following until, eventually, the incidents increase and there are fewer calm and peaceful moments, leading to continued heartache (Walker, 1979). Although this theory was developed many years ago, there is current research indicating that this type of cycle perpetuates even within narcissistic relationships, including parental narcissism (Torres, 2023), which I have been suggesting for years.

Now that we have explored power and control and the cycle of violence, take a moment to evaluate your own experiences. I have provided a visual of the cycle in Figure 10.1 to help stir your thoughts. While reviewing the

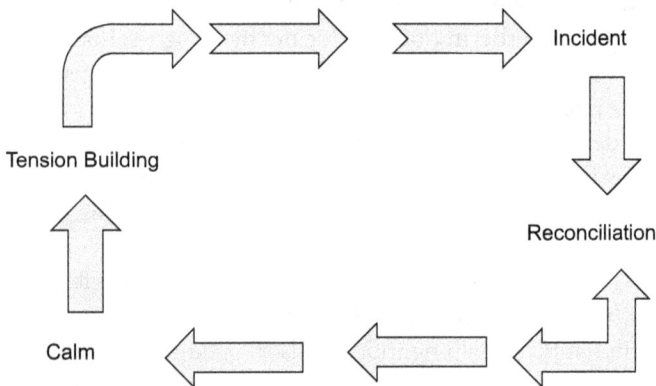

Figure 10.1 Cyle of Violence

visual, it may help you to reflect upon an experience and explore the emotional response that emerges within you as the memory unfolds.

How did you know the tension in the environment was changing?

_____

_____

_____

Describe the incident that occurred.

_____

_____

_____

What type of reconciliation was offered?

_____

_____

_____

What did the calm times look like in your life during these cycles?

_____

_____

_____

With the number of incidents in your life, you probably experienced a range of emotions along with the heightened sense of distress. When we are distressed, we often feel overwhelmed, and spurred by those feelings, we behave in ways to help reduce our distress. This can manifest in a variety of ways, such as adhering to the demands of the abuser in an attempt to de-escalate, avoiding conflict, and a plethora of other behaviors. These attempts comprise our efforts to interrupt the cycle, but understand this: this chosen behavior might temporarily stop the feeling of distress or interrupt the cycle, however, remember that you cannot control or change the NPD abuser. The only thing you can control is yourself, including your behavior. The cycle will stop only when you exit the relationship, which might be a bit easier to do if the abuser is a coworker, neighbor, or colleague but is much more challenging when it is a family member. Sometimes, it does not matter if you remain inside or are outside of the relationship—the NPD behavior will continue. Why? Unlike a domestic violence abuser, where there is the potential for criminal charges, there are minimal consequences for an NPD abuser because often there aren't physical scars that prove the abuse. Their level of manipulation often elongates the cycle, but you *do* have a choice about how you respond, which can help you to reduce internal distress. We cannot fully alleviate distress, but we can learn to tolerate it.

Distress can emerge from many different situations in life. As we noted earlier, stressful situations are not good for us physiologically or psychologically. Thus, we need a way to manage heartache and distress. In the beginning we most likely attempt to manage it via the most common method: reacting. It is normal to react when someone comes after us, but over time, you likely found that it does not help long-term, as it is fruitless to try to change the NPD abuser. However, there are some useful tools available for when we feel distressed, whether that occurs within or outside the NPD relationship. We often forget that our experiences in that environment trickle over into other parts of our lives too.

When we are pushed into a corner either figuratively or literally, we can use the skill of assertiveness. But there are times when we may need another tool for managing it, as being assertive to a NPD abuser does not work often. Consider picturing a stop sign. Bear with me on this. If I only asked you to picture a stop sign, the simplistic nature of this request would have no impact, but breaking down the letters as a method of reducing distress is quite useful.

S: Stop yourself from reacting. Literally, freeze in the moment. Stay in control of your emotions. Reacting to your abuser will not change anything. It will not suddenly make them empathetic, and it will not stop the behavior.

T: Take a step back from the situation, breathe deeply, and do not act impulsively. Refer to the story in an earlier chapter where I taught my students to stop, breathe, and proceed.

O: Observe what is happening within and outside of your body. Consider the situation, consider your thoughts and feelings, and consider what the other person is doing. This is an important step in acknowledging that your feelings are valid while taking action to not allow yourself to escalate. Your willingness to open your own awareness does not justify the other person's behavior, but it does give you an opportunity to get grounded.

P: Proceed mindfully. When proceeding mindfully, consider your goals alongside the reality that you cannot make the NPD abuser change. Remember there are no winners or losers, even though your NPD abuser might believe there are. Proceeding might involve using your assertiveness skills, self-protection elements, or a mindfulness activity. It may also mean you acknowledge but not react from your emotions, enabling you to be proud of your mindful response.

As you can see, when you go beyond merely picturing the stop sign to breaking down the elements of it, by the very act of doing these steps, you are slowly reducing your level of distress and subsequent heartache. This method has been used across various theories in the field of psychology (Beck, 2005; Linehan, 2015). It is a great way to manage the pain that comes from the gut-wrenching hurt thrown at you.

Much of the heartache from the NPD relationship relates to the constant manipulation and fear utilized in the continued power/control and abuse cycle, which even includes the fear that the cycle will never end. This leads us to an element we've only discussed briefly: acceptance. We discussed it specifically with emotions, but what about acceptance regarding the reality of a person or a situation? Marsha Linehan (2015) coined the term *radical acceptance* to help individuals understand that there are times when we have absolutely no way to avoid painful emotions or events in our life. We all have situations that come into our life over which we have no control, and the only way to cope with this reality is to accept it. Let me explain. When I was diagnosed with cancer, there was nothing I could do to change that diagnosis; thus, I had to radically accept the reality of my life at that moment. Being radical, specifically regarding acceptance, means completely accepting reality with all your heart, mind, and body, without fighting it or trying to change it into something different (Linehan, 2015). When it comes to radical acceptance of your NPD abuser, I want to be clear that doing this does not mean you approve of the behavior, that you have to express compassion for the person (although you likely are quite compassionate), that you act passively, or that you don't desire change. It is merely accepting that reality is reality, that the facts are the facts. An NPD abuser has traits that are not likely to change, and they do not have the insight to understand or acknowledge their behaviors. I want to repeat this again, as survivors of NPD abuse often stay connected to their abuser because they think the person might change. *The NPD abuser's traits are not likely to change, and they lack the insight to understand or acknowledge their behaviors.* This is an important time to take a moment to journal about whether you are at a place of radical acceptance about who your NPD abuser is. I know that I kept wishing and hoping my abuser would change if I would react differently, say something different, encourage counseling in just the right way, or any plethora of things. I had to learn that seeking to reject this reality does not change the reality.

What do you need to radically accept about your NPD abuser?

———————————————————————————————————————

———————————————————————————————————————

———————————————————————————————————————

What is stopping you from accepting the reality of the person with NPD?

———————————————————————————————————————

———————————————————————————————————————

———————————————————————————————————————

Now consider practicing acceptance of your whole self, however you define that. Contemplate your mind, body, and spirit. For myself, I had to come to the place where I realized that I could not change my abuser *and* I did not have to stay within that relationship—or any relationship where I am abused. All the practices that we have explored so far in the book are ones I have practiced in my life. What I found through acceptance is that I cannot change anyone with NPD. This set me free from fear and worry, and it helped me acknowledge my own choices in relationships. I can be happy in whatever reality I am thrown into.

The old saying "Out with the old, in with the new" is very true in my life. I have always liked change, learning and experiencing new things. As I have aged, it has been great to have consistent daily routines, where I know what to expect for my day. However, when a curveball happens or plans change, I can be very flexible and adapt. I think this is something my life experiences have empowered me to do. There is no doubt that I sometimes struggle with accepting reality. There are times that I have the creeping thought (dare I say desire?) that I will wake up one day, that my life will be different, and that I will have a parental relationship like so many others I have seen in my life. Although I've accepted my reality, the presence of this thought tells me I need to do something to manage the distressing heartache right at that moment. Those moments require I find healthy ways to distract myself. We can use distracting behaviors that are unhealthy, but I want to encourage the use of helpful distracting behaviors.

Distracting behaviors help when a feeling of crisis emerges in your life and your body is physiologically responding to those distressing events. There are various useful distracting behaviors that are connected to specific activities that promote calmness. Some may include finding ways to connect with and help others, tools to foster emotional balance, and techniques that

Table 10.1. Healthy Distracting

Category	Distracting Behavior
Activity	Exercise at the gym or make pottery on a wheel
Volunteer work	Contribute proceeds of pottery selling to the local cancer fund.
Emotions	Watch shows that evoke emotions, such as a documentary, a comedy, or a love story.
Thoughts	Meditate with a focus on a phrase "I am worthy of love."
Sensations	Take a hot bath.
Coping later	Be in the moment, and journal the daily events, thoughts, and emotions.

help manage thinking patterns. Take a moment to consider the distracting activities you use to help manage stressful situations. Reflect on a few areas in your life that can contribute to healthy distraction. Review Table 10.1, which outlines categories that assist with healthy distraction. I have provided examples to assist you.

Most of us are likely accustomed to distracting behaviors that we commonly do on autopilot. We open a bag of chips and keep on eating, start with drinking a glass of wine that turns into several glasses, are inundated with spiraling and difficult-to-manage thoughts, and have overwhelming emotions and interactions that make us feel defeated. By doing a self-assessment of our own behaviors, we can begin to adapt unhealthy distracting behaviors to healthy ones. When we do not have any alternative methods, the feeling of heartache can't improve, because we do not give it a chance, then we stay in that pain. Change is not easy, but it helps to have alternative behaviors, or as I often call them, replacement behaviors (see Chapter 9).

Before concluding this chapter, I want to give you a few ideas to help when the heartache becomes too overwhelming. I call these instant relievers; they are activities I have done to help with radically accepting the moment and redirecting away from the distressing situations.

Use Your Senses

1. Use your eyes to notice five things you can see from where you are sitting, standing, or lying. You can also use your eyes to read something that lifts you up, such as a poem, a funny book, a comedy show, or nature.

2. Use your hearing to notice four sounds in the room (or even car) you are in. Your ears can also listen to music, a podcast, or the sound of the wind blowing.
3. Use your nose to recognize the smells around you. Maybe it is food being cooked, the smell of rain in the air, or of flowers outside. Consider the use of scented candles, lotion, or essential oils.
4. Use your taste to enjoy drinking your favorite hot tea or coffee or for eating candy, gum, or another favorite food. Do it mindfully.
5. Use your hands to do something you take pleasure in. You can write, draw, pet your animal, curl up in a blanket, or ask for a hug from someone you love.

Muscle Relaxation

Progressive muscle relaxation has been around for a while. This method, where you to tense a particular muscle and then relax, is quite effective when you feel distressed. Oftentimes, people resort to a commonly used sequence (see below), but it can be applied however works best for you. Prior to starting this sequence, please remember to do this while either sitting in a chair or lying down, to do it slowly, and to not overextend any muscle and cause harm. Each movement in the sequence should be held for 5 seconds before proceeding to the next step.

Sequence

1. Right hand and forearm. Make a fist with your right hand. Hold this pose for five seconds and then release.
2. Right upper arm. Bring your right forearm up to your shoulder to "make a muscle." Hold this pose for five seconds and then release.
3. Left hand and forearm. Make a fist with your left hand. Hold this pose for five seconds and then release.
4. Left upper arm. Bring your right forearm up to your shoulder to "make a muscle." Hold this pose for five seconds and then release.
6. Forehead. Raise your eyebrows as high as they will go, as though you were surprised by something. Hold this pose for five seconds and then release.
7. Eyes and cheeks. Squeeze your eyes tight shut. Hold this pose for five seconds and then release.

8. Mouth and jaw. Open your mouth as wide as you can, as you might when you are yawning. Hold this pose for five seconds and then release.
9. Neck. Face forward, and then pull your head back slowly, as though you are looking up to the ceiling. Hold this pose for five seconds and then release.
10. Shoulders. Tense the muscles in your shoulders as you bring your shoulders up toward your ears. Hold this pose for five seconds and then release.
11. Shoulder blades/back. Push your shoulder blades back, trying to almost touch them together, so that your chest is pushed forward. Hold this pose for five seconds and then release.
12. Chest and stomach. Breathe in deeply, filling up your lungs and chest with air. Hold this pose for five seconds and then release.
13. Hips and buttocks. Squeeze your buttock muscles. Hold this pose for five seconds and then release.
14. Right upper leg. Tighten your right thigh. Hold this pose for five seconds and then release.
15. Right lower leg. Pull your toes toward you to stretch the calf muscle. Hold this pose for five seconds and then release.
16. Right foot. Curl your toes downward. Hold this pose for five seconds and then release.
17. Left upper leg. Repeat what was done for the right upper leg. Hold this pose for five seconds and then release.
18. Left lower leg. Repeat what was done for the right lower leg. Hold this pose for five seconds and then release.
19. Left foot. Repeat what was done for the right foot. Hold this pose for five seconds and then release.

Quick Muscle Relievers

1. Shape your face into a "monster face," hold it for up to 30 seconds, then release it. Notice the difference in the tensing and releasing.
2. Lift both shoulders up to your ears, hold your shoulders up for up to 30 seconds, then release them.
3. Curl your fingers up, hold for up to 30 seconds, and release them.
4. Put your left hand and fingers on the left side of your head, putting pressure on that left side. Put your right hand and fingers on the right side of your head, putting pressure on that right side. You will hold this position for up to 30 seconds, then release it.

5. Put about three cups of ice in a sink, and add some cold water. The water will become icy cold. Quickly dip your head into the icy water and then pull your head out. It can be a quick rush and is what I call a quick "rewire."

6. Box breathing: Picture a box in your head or a cube. Imagine how you would draw that box. Typically, we draw the top line, right line, left line, and then bottom line. As you do this, let's slow down the process.
   a. In your mind, draw the first line of the box, and as you do this, inhale your breath.
   b. Now, in your mind, draw the right line, then exhale.
   c. Now, in your mind, draw the left line, then inhale.
   d. Now, draw the bottom line, then exhale.
   e. Keep imagining the box, and do this inhale-and-exhale sequence.

7. Exercise/quick movement
   a. Make a plan to do cardio work at least three times a week with weight lifting on at least two of the days. Weight lifting reduces depression and anxiety (Hooda et al., 2024).
   b. Do five quick jumping jacks.
   c. Plant an herb, flower, or vegetable in a box garden.
   d. Walk briskly for 10 minutes.
   e. Take your shoes off, and walk on soft grass for 5 minutes.
   f. Do 10 of the head, shoulders, knees, and toes moves we did as a kid.
   g. Dance to your favorite song.

Heartache and pain are a natural part of the human experience. However, they can be felt more frequently within an NPD abusive relationship. The pain is persistent because the cycle, just like with interpersonal violence, increases and gets worse over time. When a cycle like this continues to grow and unfold, you now have some tools to assist you in managing these distressing situations. I know it seems frustrating that you almost always have to be the one to manage the NPD abuser's behaviors. However, remember that they lack insight into their problem, but you have a clear perception. They very seldom change, but *you* can change. Do what is best for your own mental health because you are worth it.

CHAPTER 11

~

Embrace the Light

Leaning Into Spiritual Elements That Support Healing

I identify as a spiritual person. This has not always been true for me, since I grew up in a Christian home with parents who identified as Christian, but the behaviors I associated with being Christian varied across my life. There were times that we rarely, if ever, went to church. I remember attending church on major holidays as a family and, at other times, being dropped off alone to attend the children and youth activities. This was my life until I was 12 years old, and then our lives completely changed. My father announced that he felt called to the ministry. This created quite a shift in our family.

During the time I was finishing middle school and high school and then heading into college, I was on my own spiritual journey. I never quite felt connected to organized religion. Of course, I attended my father's church even during the times I'd have preferred to stay home. And as I met my now husband in high school, I attended his church at times as well. After marriage, my husband, children, and I attended, participated, and volunteered across several types of denominations, but I always felt disconnected. It was not until I began the process of evaluating my belief in a higher power, my internal spirit and soul, and our universal connection that I found my path. For me, that path is a spiritual one, where I believe in God and practice journaling, prayer, mindfulness, universal kindness, and love for others. I believe that we all have a soul and a spirit along with a powerful intuition that we can access at any time. Intuition has guided my decision-making, helped spark my creativity, fostered my confidence, and kept me from harm. This personal journey has helped me to accept myself more and to feel my spiritual connection to people, animals, and all things in the universe. I have no expectations for others to believe as I do. We all have the right to our own spiritual beliefs. Therefore, it is important for you to determine what religious/spiritual or nonreligious/spiritual aspects are a part of your life. Why would I inquire about this? This is an especially important topic given that a 2023 Gallup poll showed that over 80% of Americans chose to identify with some type of belief system, whether religious or spiritual (Jones, 2023). Your spirituality and religious beliefs vary based on a multitude of factors, though this does not negate the topic's importance, and it should be addressed. This chapter focuses on considering your spiritual or religious beliefs and examining elements of wellness in your life. Exposure to NPD abuse can erase your sense of self, which includes your loss of purpose and meaning. As part of self-validating, you first need to know your personally held beliefs. Knowing these will help you effectively navigate what forgiveness means for you personally and for your NPD abuser. Your beliefs shape your perception of forgiveness. Sometimes, part of this reflective process includes exploring how to grieve the old self and embrace the new you. When you focus on these areas intentionally, the light can shine in through dark periods.

You have completed a lot of self-evaluations throughout this book, and now it is time to assess your own personally held beliefs around spirituality and religion. I have a few questions for you to reflect on and answer to start off your identification process.

Do you identify with a particular faith tradition or religious or spiritual belief? Whether you answered yes or no, please explain further.

_____

_____

_____

What was your spiritual and religious background in childhood?

_____

_____

_____

How has this background influenced you today?

_____

_____

_____

What do you spend most of your day doing?

_____

_____

_____

What gives your life meaning?

_____

_____

_____

What helps you cope in times of stress or illness?

_____

_____

_____

In what ways do you apply your faith in your daily life?

_____

_____

_____

What do you believe about the afterlife, and how did this belief develop?

_____

_____

_____

What do you believe about forgiveness?

_____

_____

_____

Whether you do or do not have any religious or spiritual beliefs, these questions regarding meaning and how to handle stress provide a window into what you believe. What we spend most of our lives doing reflects our values, for our activities often reflect our priorities. This might be work, family, or even education, as noted in an earlier chapter. These questions help you to determine your beliefs. Our beliefs will drive our behavior and are commonly influenced by how we were raised. But our own development over time has also contributed to these beliefs; they drive us and set up our lives' priorities, which speaks to their powerful purpose.

As a counselor and counselor-educator, I have long promoted client and student wellness. From the early 1990s through today, Myers et al. (2000) studied the factors that promote wellness in clients. I am proud of the viewpoint counselors hold, which promotes a holistic approach to treatment. We cannot merely focus on career, emotional, physical, or psychological wellness; we must focus on all aspects of the self, including spirituality. According to Myers et al. (2000), spirituality was considered as both a core factor of healthy people and a primary element of all other characteristics of wellness (Chandler et al., 1992; Seward, 1995). There are multiple aspects to spirituality, including what it holds for meaningfulness and inner peace (Kauppi et al., 2023). Of course, folks define spirituality in different ways, depending upon their beliefs, but the fact remains that spiritual tenets promote wellness. Thus, it is worth considering what that means for your life and then find ways to promote it, as elements of spirituality can nurture a sense of purpose and meaning during life's challenging events (e.g., exposure to an NPD abuser). It can be challenging to admit the power that our NPD abuser has over even our concept of belief. I know that I was very influenced. My family was integrated into the Christian community. The way my family acted prior to attending church and then the changes that occurred upon their arriving or leaving the church building shaped many aspects of my life. Raised a Christian, I was taught to forgive and am very forgiving, but I was also taught to "forget" and give folks second chances. As a result, no matter how badly I was treated, I would forgive and consider each day as a new start and a clean slate for the person. Unfortunately, this was not the best option for me, as it perpetuated my NPD abuse. I would not only forgive, but I'd provide excuses for the behaviors exhibited toward me, which only justified the abuse. It was not until I grew to adulthood that I understood that forgiveness does not have to mean forgetting. I had to rewire my thinking about the concept of forgiving and forgetting. Forgiving does not mean that I must continue to put myself into an abusive environment as a means of demonstrating that have forgiven the person. I have found that to have a sense of peace and what I call spiritual soundness, it is essential for me to understand forgiveness, recognize its importance, and ultimately forgive my NPD abuser. Fincham (2022) reiterated that forgiveness is a common principle across world religions and is included in the behaviors of specific doctrine.

What is forgiveness? There are varied viewpoints on forgiveness that approach it from different perspectives: religious, spiritual, secular, and mental health. Psychologists explore the definition of forgiveness from a behavioral perspective, which includes acting. Many reiterate that forgiving goes beyond a reduction of anger or resentment over what happened to not allowing your emotions to dominate your life. Most definitions of forgiveness include the common element of releasing resentment. Forgiveness has been defined as "the action of forgiving; pardon of a fault, remission of a debt, etc." (Oxford English Dictionary, 2023). Another way to consider forgiveness is as the "willingness to abandon one's right to resentment, negative judgment and indifferent behavior toward one who unjustly hurts us, while fostering the undeserved qualities of compassion, generosity, and even love toward him or her" (Enright et al., 1998, p. 47). Anderson et al. (2006) explored how forgiveness is a process that can take some time and needs to be both intentional and voluntary in order to actually forgive the person who has offended or caused harm. They also add an element reinforcing that the victim should be is fully aware that they deserve(d) to be treated better. This is how I see forgiveness.

Choose two from what is likely many definitions of forgiveness, read them, and then take a minute to ask yourself how you would define forgiveness. Consider what being forgiven or forgiving others means to you. I'd gone to therapy several times, and there was only one counselor who addressed me with a compassionate tone regarding my exposure to NPD abuse while treading cautiously on the concept of forgiveness. Many folks, even trained professionals, approach forgiveness from a religious lens, using the concept of forgive and forget—as if I hadn't forgiven my NPD abuser. I would say, "I have forgiven." And then they'd add the question, "Well, did you forget?" Truth be told, I do not want to forget. Furthermore, how can I when what I've experienced has shaped my whole existence and likely impacted my thoughts about self, my interactions with others, and my concept of trust? I challenge you to consider the perception you have of the idea of "forgive and forget."

There have been different theories regarding forgiveness as well. Walrond-Skinner (1998) conducted a deep dive of seven different types of forgiveness, each of which had varying contexts surrounding how an individual reacts to a transgression. The seven types include a false form of forgiveness where the harmful act is denied or forgotten very quickly, forgiveness that is completely denied by the victim and perpetrator, forgiveness that is only given under specific circumstances, forgiveness to merely restore a relationship, forgiveness that happens to avoid conflict, repeated forgiveness given although the behaviors continue, and then authentic forgiveness, where revenge is not sought and there is an altruistic desire to let go of the transgression (Walrond-Skinner, 1998).

Additional concepts associated with forgiveness are forgetting, excusing, pardoning, and denying (Enright & Coyle, 1998), and others have hypothesized about the existence of additional forms of forgiveness, such as forgiveness motivated by revenge, motivated due to social pressure, motivated by the goal of fostering a sense of peace and harmony, and motivated by the desire to align with lawful duty (Enright et al., 1989). As you can see, there have been multiple attempts at trying to understand what forgiveness is, but I do think we need to also consider what forgiveness is not. Please review Table 11.1, which outlines the difference between the two.

Why should anyone forgive another? I know that some individuals say they can never forgive someone for what was done to them. I think about those individuals who have experienced the murder of a loved one, sexual assault, severe abuse, and other unimaginable things. I know that if I faced this experience in my life, I'd find forgiveness very difficult, especially when it comes to someone in my own family being hurt. However, forgiveness promotes psychological well-being (Akhtar & Barlow, 2018). If we think about it practically, we need to be connected to individuals, and thus all of our

Table 11.1. What Forgiveness Is and Is Not

What Forgiveness Is	What Forgiveness Is Not
A commitment to not dwell on the incident mentally (overthinking and overanalyzing)	Forgetting what happened
A commitment to letting go of the emotions that have kept you trapped	Excusing what was done to you
A commitment to awareness that what happened was wrong but that you need to let it go for your own mental, emotional, and psychological well-being	Trusting the offender
A commitment to being aware that people can disappoint us and hurt us and that we do not have to allow that in our lives	Accepting the wrong done to you
A commitment to relieving yourself of the pain of feeling that if you'd done something different, then the offense would not have happened	Tolerance.
A commitment to taking back your power and not allowing the offense to occupy your time, attention, and life	Relieving the person of responsibility

relationships will have both good and bad situations and outcomes. There are many times when we have to seek out forgiveness or need to forgive. However, within an NPD abusive relationship, this dynamic is heightened, as the behaviors accumulate over many years. We need relationships, and yet our relationships can be a high source of pain in our lives (Van Tongeren et al., 2015). Relationships can be a source of joy as well, but when something challenging happens, it's easy for us to fixate on the difficult moments. We must be cognizant that when we are connected with an NPD abuser, there are more difficult times than there would be in an average relationship.

We may not have a reason to forgive our NPD abuser (their behaviors haven't changed) except that there are benefits for the forgiver. Since relationships are part of the human experience, we derive meaning from them, but when we experience a disruption in a relationship, this often deteriorates the relationship quality and disrupts harmony (Worthington, 2005). Thus, there is a critical need to get back to that harmony and have relational repair, which comes from forgiving. Practicing forgiveness even benefits us by enhancing our sense of meaning and self-esteem (Van Tongeren et al., 2015). Therefore, think about the varied ways forgiveness benefits you, not the perpetrator. Before reading further, think about times when you have forgiven. How did you feel because of it? I've been hurt by many individuals beyond my NPD abuser. It can be gut-wrenching when someone you trust has betrayed you, but when I was able to forgive them, I felt a sense of relief. I want to remind you that forgiveness does not require you go up to the perpetrator and say you forgive them. In fact, you can forgive someone after they have passed away (showing it is possible at a distance). Let's examine how forgiveness can help you.

1. When you enact forgiveness, you also recognize the importance of others forgiving you for small or large transgressions. We all have moments when we need forgiveness, whether it is due to a small lie we told, an angry outburst we had, or other transgressions (minor or major) we've committed throughout our lives.

2. When you forgive, you take back your power. When you do not forgive, you are metaphorically allowing that person to have a hold on you mentally, emotionally, psychologically, and spiritually. You can forgive someone and never see them again. When you forgive, you are no longer a victim but a survivor, and you slowly become stronger and stronger when releasing the negative energy of the perpetrator.

3. When you forgive, your health benefits. When we have anxiety, anger, and stress, our bodies are impacted through high blood pressure and/

or heart rate and worse outcomes of mental health distress. When we forgive, we can experience a type of reversal of these health problems. We can lower our levels of anxiety, stress, and hostility. This then lowers our blood pressure, improves our sleeping, decreases the depth of our depression, and lowers our risk of substance abuse. It is important that we do not allow our lack of forgiveness to cause us medical problems.

4. Forgiveness provides us peace and reduces the dramatic cycle. When we forgive, we demonstrate our empathy and compassion. This compassion is for us, because our simmering in resentment does nothing to change an NPD abuser. Remember that the abuser does not care about and so will never acknowledge their wrongdoing, but you can be at peace knowing that you are enhancing peace in your life. As we consider the spiritual self as core, we can have greater spiritual and psychological well-being.

5. Forgiveness promotes healthier relationships and trust. It can be hard to trust, but we are able to learn what is considered a healthy relationship in comparison to an unhealthy one, and you can provide appropriate boundaries for those who are impacting you negatively. We want more individuals who bring in joy and light versus pain and darkness.

Because we know what forgiveness is and why it is important, we need to consider the process of forgiveness. There are several theories about forgiveness and how to approach the process. I do like the model proposed by Enright (2012) because it acknowledges that clients go through phases in the process of forgiveness, and it expands upon his seminal work regarding forgiveness being a choice (Enright, 2001). I do agree that forgiveness is an action and a choice. When we make a choice, we behave in a way that depicts our choice. Let's examine his theory, and as I break down the content, I invite you to explore where you are in the forgiveness process.

Prior to examining the phases of forgiveness proposed by Enright (2012), answer the following questions:

1. Who hurt you?

_____

2. How deeply were you hurt by this person?

_____

_____

_____

3. What specific incident will you focus on? It is important to break down each incident where you need to forgive, not unlike the typical hierarchy of trauma. It is important to focus on one at a time.

_____

_____

_____

4. What were the circumstances surrounding the situation? Provide details about what was said and how the day was (morning or afternoon, sunny or cloudy), and consider how you responded to the situation.

_____

_____

_____

After addressing each of these questions, the process of forgiveness can begin. Enright (2012) proposed that forgiveness begins with the uncovering phases, then moves into the decision phase, the phases about working on forgiveness, and then, finally, the deepening phase. Breaking down each of these phases would benefit you as you contemplate your NPD abuser.

Uncovering Phase

During this phase you are evaluating the emotional pain that has resulted due to the injury. This is commonly explored in the form of anger, but it can appear as other negative emotions. Take a minute to assess what emotion(s) you have experienced because of the chosen offense. After you consider the emotion(s), it is important to further break down the emotions and assess them.

1. How have you avoided dealing with this emotion (e.g., anger)?

_____

2. Have you faced this emotion? If so, how?

_____

_____

3. Are you afraid to expose this emotion? Why?

_____

_____

4. How has this emotion impacted your health?

_____

_____

5. Have you been obsessed with the injury or the offender? If so, how?

_____

_____

6. How do you compare your situation with that of the offender?

_____

_____

_____

7. How has this injury caused permanent change in your life?

_____

_____

_____

8. How has the injury changed your worldview?

_____

_____

_____

Decision Phase

In the decision phase, you begin to realize that focusing on this person who has caused you the injury and/or focusing on the injury itself will cause more harm and suffering for you. In this process you may begin to see how forgiving is beneficial to your own physiological and mental wellness. In other words, you are at a point where you are deciding to forgive. Typically, this decision is connected to evaluating how what you have been doing so far, as noted in the uncovering phase, has not worked. Thus, you are at a point of beginning the forgiveness process and are ready to work on forgiving. Ask yourself, What will make me ready to decide to forgive my NPD abuser?

Working on Forgiveness

The working phase is, as you can imagine, one where you must work. Work can be fun, but most of the time, it is stressful and can even be overwhelming. In this phase you are beginning the active work of forgiving. The first part of this phase is working toward understanding. When you work to understand, this is not you excusing the person or the injury they caused; however, this is when you attempt to understand the context regarding why the offense happened. It is very likely that individuals with NPD had dysfunctional childhoods. Is this something you need to consider? In my own life, I have often considered this. It does not excuse the ongoing offenses, but it does shed light on why my offender has perpetuated her harmful behaviors. I have found that when I do this, I feel more compassion and empathy for the offender. This does not discount the pain I experienced from her defenses and attacks toward me, but it allows me to understand and release my need to defend myself. I know I did not do anything wrong, but trying to stand up against the offender is pointless. Remember: NPD abusers do not see their behaviors as troubling. There is so much pain in facing the reality of the ongoing lies, manipulations, and hurtful attacks you received, so your acceptance of the pain is critical. When you are working on forgiveness, you might desire to tell the offender that you forgive them, but remember that it is not likely to be acknowledged. You can offer this "gift" of forgiveness at a distance. Instead, you could engage a process of journaling and meditation that releases the pain. There is even an option available that's called a loving-kindness meditation. One of the steps in this meditation asks us to consider sending positive energy to those who are difficult to love. Sending that out into the universe can be very powerful.

Deepening Phase

The deepening phase brings a physiological release and sense of relief, enabling you to free yourself from your emotional pain, akin to having carried a heavy bag on your back for ages and finally getting to take it off. You feel a sense of relief that the weight has been lifted. When you forgive your NPD abuser and offer them a sense of compassion and empathy, you are healing as well. With this process you realize you are not alone in your pain, that you and others suffer, and that forgiveness can be very freeing. Forgiveness frees you from all responsibility for the offense—analyzing the reason the person has offended and holding on to it—all is gone.

I know these phases will take some time, but I encourage you to risk the process of forgiveness. As your understanding deepens, you will begin to feel a more profound sense of relief in your life. This does not mean you will forget the offenses. In fact, you need to remember them so you do not get ensnared in the dramatic cycle again. You are led to grieve the relationship you did not (or do not) have with your NPD abuser. To some extent you might have realized the unhealthy nature of the cycle at the time, but it was familiar to you and thus easy to perpetuate.

We stay in relationships because we hope that the situation will change or the person will suddenly grow to be enlightened and change. Realistically, change is not that easy, and now we know the nature of NPD is that it does not change. We can wait time and time again for a person to be different, but my work in counseling and psychology consistently proves how irrational this is. We cannot make anyone change, and when there is a formal NPD diagnosis, change is fleeting and will do no good. The truth is that if we cannot influence change with this personality, we must accept it as is. With that acceptance, we can move forward to face the heightened level of grief we will experience.

Even today I grieve several things connected to my NPD abuser. I grieve the authentic love I wish I'd received as a person but also, more importantly, as a daughter. I grieve what never was and will never be in my life. I grieve that I did not and will never encounter praise, love, and acknowledgment of what I have accomplished. I really would love to hear, "I am proud of you." I grieve that I did not and will never hear those words. I grieve for the healthy parental support that should have been there for me when I got married, graduated from college, had children, and was diagnosed with cancer. None of these loving dynamics ever existed in my life, so I've had to face the different points in my life when the grief has hit me. I ask you to step back and consider your own grief regarding this relationship. I am aware that your NPD abuser may be a friend, family member, romantic partner, coworker, colleague, and/or a parent. There are many types of relationships that can be affected by NPD abuse. Before I was able to recognize the NPD abuse in my life, I unfortunately ended up connecting with too many people who had NPD. As I look back, I give myself grace, as that was all I knew, and thus, I gravitated to them. I am sure they energetically connected to me as well. Take a minute to consider what you need to grieve. By acknowledging what you need to grieve, you pull yourself out of the darkness and begin to see the light in your life.

CHAPTER 12

∽

You Have a Choice

It feels good to sit in a brand-new car or house or even in something that's been freshly cleaned. It feels pure for a moment, but then it eventually becomes dirty and beaten up, needing to be cleaned again. We are capable of understanding the difference between old and new objects, but we do not give ourselves permission to be renewed as a human being. Sometimes, we think we are far too tarnished or damaged to ever have a sense of purity again. We may think we have gone too far to turn back or change our path in life. However, I challenge you to question the old self, the you prior to picking up this book, and begin to see the new you that is emerging.

When we get something new, we often throw out or give away the old item. We trade in an old car for a new one, older or out-of-style clothes for the latest fashions, and an old house for building or buying newer or bigger. Our society really values the newest, the latest, and the best, which is one reason why we have so much trash and so many consignment shops. Thankfully, even when something may be considered old to one person, someone else can discover and appreciate it. I really enjoy going to consignment shops, garage sales, and even auctions. I love to look at an old piece of furniture and think about the stories the object holds. It is amazing to think about all the history we've lived across our lives. Those lived experiences are powerful. As a teacher and a counselor, I've come to value everyone's lived experiences because we all have a story, and some folks have been through more in their lives than their chronological age would indicate. It is important to remind you to value your lived experiences.

What are lived experiences? These refer to all the accumulated knowledge about the world you have gained through direct, firsthand involvement in everyday events and through connections with people via direct interaction: all your experiences at work, at home, and in social environments, as well as all of your connections to peers, family, and intimate partners. All these experiences are part of your life story, and it may be that these stories reveal the times you were potentially at fault for an outcome, and they may reveal the times others were at fault. Remember: you are human, and we all make mistakes. I imagine that if you've gone back and forth about how to manage the relationship with your NPD abuser, you've likely wanted to stand up for yourself, protect yourself, walk away from the situation, or permanently disconnect from your NPD abuser. We can always look back on our situations with regret, but we can also learn from those situations—and we often learn more from failures than from success. Our lives are full of lessons, and with these lessons, we can choose to look back and regret our choices, be proud of our choices, live in regret, or be willing to move past it. I am asking you to take the lessons, learn from them, and now take a step toward a new you. You can start over at any time and be a different person. This chapter explores the options that survivors have for their future, such as remaining intertwined with the person with NPD or moving beyond the relationship. I explore ways to tame the cognitive automatic thoughts, to live beyond the guilt, to navigate choices regarding these NPD relationships, and finally, to live as the person you were meant to be. Before I delve into the choice-making process, take a minute to consider some thought-provoking questions regarding your identity. These can be a catalyst for you to continue making positive changes in your life:

What turning points have you experienced in your life? Consider listing those.

_____

_____

What did these turning points evoke within you?

_____

_____

What brings joy into your life?

_____

_____

Where do you find the most meaning in your life?

_____

_____

What lasting impact do you want to make in the world, and with whom?

_____

_____

_____

What is stopping you from taking a positive risk in your life?

_____

_____

_____

What is your greatest fear?

_____

_____

_____

How can you transform the inner longings held within your mind and heart into action?

_____

_____

_____

Most important, what is one thing you can do in your life as a demonstration of your own

_____

_____

self-love?

_____

_____

I end with the question about self-love because, even if all the other questions were difficult to answer, you can choose one thing to demonstrate self-love. When I started working on loving myself, my first step was telling myself, "I am good enough." That developed slowly into more powerful statements, and then I believed these thoughts, which later manifested into action. Those actions were sometimes scary, but they were powerful and empowering. We all must make a choice, and it can be hard when what you need to do involves the potential severing of a relationship or, at the very least, introducing a big shift into a relationship. Let's discuss choice theory as a part of helping you decide your next steps.

I had the honor many years ago to meet William Glasser at a state conference. I'd learned about the development of his theory, called choice theory, while I was in graduate school. However, it all seemed to come full circle when I connected with him in person at the conference. He lived, breathed, and genuinely followed the tenets outlined in his theory. It seems like a simple concept, but it goes far deeper than merely making choices. Choice theory delves into the various facets that contribute to making choices. A primary factor reiterated throughout the theory is that the only true thing any of us can control is ourselves. We cannot control others, and we certainly cannot do anything about those with NPD. When taking control of your own life, you no longer see the need to influence other decisions. It is a theory that encourages self-empowerment (Glasser, 2013).

When you have control over your own life, the purpose driving your behaviors is to get what you want. Getting what you want helps you satisfy one of several basic needs. These needs relate to the basic needs of survival, which include what we learned in grade school about the need for food, shelter, water, clothing, air, and light. If that were all we needed, that would be a limited life, but of course we need other things as well. The other needs that Glasser (1999) explores are the need for love and belonging, power, freedom, and fun. However, it is very difficult to focus on these additional needs if we our basic needs for survival have not been met. Someone who has not eaten in several days may not be very concerned about seeking out a sense of power. Breaking down each of these needs is a valuable tool to help us begin to see the importance of all of these areas of need.

Our basic needs include those things in life that we, as humans, typically think everyone has the right to so they may sustain their lives. Most governments provide some form of assistance for those who are struggling to maintain these needs. There are programs for assistance with food, housing, and work. However, there is still a great unmet need to assist women and children, especially women who are single mothers or displaced homemakers.

There are even grants available for individuals to start programs that will assist with these varied needs in our world. Unfortunately, there will always be folks who are deprived of their basic needs in life. It breaks my heart to know that we have enough food to feed everyone, and yet there are children and adults starving.

When we have met our basic needs, according to Glasser (1999), we feel safe and secure. I think back to when Hurricane Katrina hit Mississippi and Louisiana. I was doing crisis counseling in the shelters, and there were so many displaced individuals within our community that we first had to ensure their basic needs were met before we could then jump in and begin to counsel them. These individuals had no idea if they would ever go back home, and if they did, whether they would even have a place to live. When you think about your life, do you remember if there was ever a time you struggled for any of your basic needs? If so, I am sure it is an overwhelming memory—or it might be your present reality. Many individuals are only one paycheck away from poverty or homelessness. If you've never struggled with obtaining and maintaining your basic needs, I may be difficult to relate to what a struggle that would be for someone, though I'm sure you can imagine it is terrible. It is heartbreaking to think about someone not having food or water, much less a place for shelter in bad weather. Hopefully, I have effectively describe the importance of meeting our basic needs in life prior being able to delve into our other human needs. Consider this: someone has not had food in several days and comes over to your office to see you. They are overwhelmed by the smell of a box of leftovers in the trash. How could they think about anything else but food? Their mind can only focus on that and nothing else. But if those basic needs are met, then we can begin to investigate the other needs laid out by Glasser (1999; 2013): love and belonging, power, freedom, and fun.

Love and belonging are something that most people strive to bring into their lives. We desire relating with others, such as our friends, family, intimate partners, coworkers, pets, and social interest groups. This is not a new idea, as it has been historically addressed by earlier researchers, including Moreno (1934), who explored the social relationships of people within and between groups, as well as how these relations can be beneficial to and potentially harm humans. We as human beings can do countless different things to promote or hinder relationships, which may seem obvious after your exposure to NPD abuse. We can demonstrate either helpful or harmful relationship habits, based on our behavioral approaches. Ask yourself, What do I do to obtain love and belonging in my life? For some folks, it comes very easily, while it can be quite difficult for others. In Table 12.1, I break down

Table 12.1. Effective and Ineffective Relationship Behaviors

Effective Relationship Behaviors	Ineffective Relationship Behaviors
Supporting	Criticizing or bribing
Encouraging	Blaming
Listening	Complaining
Accepting	Nagging
Trusting	Threatening
Respecting	Punishing
Accepting and understanding differences	Seeking control

some effective and ineffective relationship behaviors that you may exhibit or have seen in your NPD abuser.

Consider the variety within these two categories of relationship behaviors. Which ones do you value? Which ones drew you closer to your NPD abuser? Which ones push you further from your NPD abuser? These are important to consider because you have the power to choose what and who you would like in your life. Of course, our choices are often driven by what we perceive we need to be happy, so it's essential to take an honest look at what we actually have in our lives. I come back to explain this later in this chapter. But before we explore this, it is first important to examine the next area of need: power.

When we think of the definition of power, we often picture someone seeking to control or overtake another. Additionally, this may come to mind since this book is about defeating the narcissistic giant. Glasser (1999; 2013) perceived power in a different context. He found it critically important to help people find what matters in their lives. This is about assessing what you do well, how you can make a difference in life, and what your skills, strengths, and areas of competence are in your life. You can also examine it by asking about what boosts your self-esteem. I think back to a child in elementary school who gets to be the star student for the day. On their day they get to be the line leader, wear a beautiful star, bring their favorite toy to school, and get doted on for the day. This can feel very good, especially when you're getting recognized, but what if you never have a sense of this kind of power? What if you've never felt special, competent, or capable of anything specific in your life? What if there is a complete lack of meaningfulness? In your life within the context of the NPD relationship, you have likely been overshadowed by your NPD abuser, as they've always required you make them feel like the special one. If this has been true for you, you've been thrown into the shadows, living behind the scenes. It may feel like that is an okay place to be, but Glasser (1999; 2013) encouraged everyone

to find their power within. Ask yourself a few questions to assess your level
of power.

What have you accomplished on your own that no one can take away
from you?

_____

_____

In which areas of your life do you have a sense of self-confidence?

_____

_____

What is your level of self-esteem (0 being none, 10 being the highest)?

_____

Once you have provided a number, express what that number means to
you, then choose a number that represents where you would like to be
within the next year.

_____

_____

How can you get to this number?

_____

_____

Your answers to these questions are critically important because we all
need to feel special sometimes. And when you are within an NPD abusive
relationship, you likely have been broken down, with your self-esteem at its
lowest, and you are not sure how to bring yourself back up. Please remember
that you have a choice, that you can change at any time. This choice can
begin right now, which is where the need for freedom comes into the picture.

The last two needs are surrounding freedom and fun. Freedom is another
need that is often misunderstood by individuals. It is easy to think of patrio-
tism. Some may even think about the power of free will with a wink and a
smile, as though free will was not possible. Glasser (1999; 2013) argued that
we do actually have free will, but he called it choices. He reiterated that we
all can achieve independence and autonomy in our lives by the choices that
we make. He also talked about how freedom means that humans have the

right to move around freely, without restriction. You are likely thinking, "What? I always feel restricted." If you do feel restricted, it's time to do an honest self-evaluation about your life, including your relationships, work, hobbies, and so forth. When we feel truly free, we support our own choices, are creative with our ideas, and form opinions. Take a moment and ask yourself, What decisions do I get to make in my life? Some individuals feel stifled, with no power to make even minimal decisions, so let's start very small. What choices did you get to make today? I know that one choice you made was to pick up this book and read it. Another choice might be in how you combed your hair or the fact that you brushed your teeth. These decisions can get even larger, working up through your choice in college major. Take some time to evaluate what choices you've gotten to make in your life, and then, using Table 12.2, consider what you do because you've been required or were pressured.

Now that you have outlined these two columns, consider if some of your pressured choices can be eliminated—or even just adjusted in some way—by implementing the skills you have used in this book. I know you have already learned so much about yourself on this journey to defeat the NPD giant in your life so that you can begin your own life. The final need that Glasser (1999; 2013) explained was the need for fun in our lives. When was the last time you had fun? Right now, as I write this, I am listening to Adele's *21* album and singing along. That is fun to me, and there are so many different things in my life that I really enjoy. Think about the things in your life that bring you pleasure, make you laugh and feel relaxed, where you get to be playful and just smile. I take little moments throughout each of my days to do that. Even after I have a late-night class, I will come home and watch a funny show or play a board game with my family. I am very hopeful that you, too, do things for fun. Sometimes, as we get older, we feel as if we must

Table 12.2. Personal Versus Pressured Choices

Personal Choices	Pressured Choices

be serious, that fun is no longer an option. Well, you need fun in your life! And it's important to give yourself permission to do at least one fun thing a week. Heck, you can even do one fun thing a day.

You now know the importance of meeting basic needs for survival as well as of love and belonging, power, freedom, and fun, but Glasser (1999; 2013) explained that this is not enough: it is not sufficient to only know about these needs, but we also need to go a step further to understand the difference between what we would like to have in our lives and what we already have. He reiterated that we have the potential to get what we want in our lives but added that we should ask ourselves, What has come to my mind and heart that I have often wished I had? Glasser (1999; 2013) called this your quality world, which lives within every person's mind and holds people, places, things, values, and beliefs that are important for you (sometimes known as magical thinking). Each person's quality world is different from another's, which is why it is not likely you will see eye to eye about the same wants when you compare your needs to others'. Alas, we live in the real world and not in this quality world, but even in the real world, our individual perspective determines how we interact within it. We interpret the world based on our experiences, which we take in through what we see, hear, taste, smell, and touch. The five senses are very powerful and may contribute to creating lasting memories that hinder us from moving forward and thus stifle our choices (Glasser, 1999; 2013). For an example, consider the following scenario: in your quality world, you really want a loving partner who listens to you, but in the real world, your partner talks over you and minimizes your opinions. Well, you are not getting what you want, so there is a disconnect between what you would like to have and what you actually have in your life, creating a painful disconnect. The behaviors we choose are influenced by many factors; for example, if we got what we wanted, we would continue to feel great, and our behavior would not change. If we experience a continual disconnect in our minds, bodies, and spirits, we'll want to make steps toward change. To work toward obtaining what you want, you must assess four areas: wants, doing (or direction), evaluation, and plan of action (WDEP).

William Glasser (1999; 2013) explained that this formula can be a great help in discovering and identifying what you want, in exploring what you are doing to get what you want, in evaluating if your actions are actually helping or hurting your ability to effectively get what you want, and then in considering how to make an effective plan of action. I have used this formula both in my life and with many clients across my career and have found it to be very beneficial. But first, is it is helpful to describe these areas a bit more so there can be a broader sense of what they mean in your life and in relation to an

NPD relationship. It is a good idea to think of the steps in this process using the WDEP acronym.

Consider all the information we have shared about our basic needs in life, and keep the need for love, power, freedom, and fun at hand as you consider your *wants*.

What do you want out of the relationship with the person with NPD?

_____

_____

What need did you think your NPD relationship would fulfill in your life (e.g., love, power, freedom, fun, other)?

_____

_____

What is the picture you had in your mind (in your quality world) that you thought you would have in this real-world relationship?

_____

_____

Now it is time to consider in which direction this NPD abusive relationship is taking you with the following assessment, made up of several questions. In this "doing" assessment, Glasser (1999; 2013) called this *total behavior* because it refers to how we act, what we are thinking, what we are feeling, and what is unfolding physiologically in our bodies as part of the doing and direction aspect.

What have you been *doing* to get what you want from the NPD relationship? Examine each component, and I will provide an example to give you a sense of what your answer could look like. After you review each of the areas and my example, take an honest assessment of these four areas and write your response.

Acting: (begging to be understood)

_____

_____

Thinking: (worrying about or remembering the good times)

_____

_____

Feeling: (anxious)

_____

_____

Physiological: (headaches)

_____

_____

All four of these components together dictate the direction the relationship has gone in the past or will continue to go in the future. Thus, the next step is *evaluating* these elements, which will help you decide your plan of action.

Is what you are doing (regarding your acting, thinking, feeling, and physiology) helping you get what you want in this NPD relationship?

_____

Is the relationship taking you in the direction you want to go in the future?

_____

_____

Is this NPD relationship hindering you in some way? If so, how?

_____

_____

How necessary is it for you to remain in this NPD relationship?

_____

_____

How is your current level of commitment to this NPD relationship working for you?

_____

_____

Do you have a plan of action on how to manage this NPD relationship?

_____

_____

Is it a helpful plan?

_____

_____

Are you willing to reevaluate your plan?

_____

These questions are important because it is now time to consider the final area of Glasser's (1999; 2013) model, the *plan* of action. Remember that in choice theory, the whole purpose is to empower you to be able to make choices that impact your life and to help you successfully achieve what you want. Thus, here is the final set of questions to be used in exploring your current and future plans of action:

What are you prepared to do or think differently to take you in the direction you want to go for a healthy relationship?

_____

_____

_____

Do you clearly understand what you are going to do about the NPD relationship?

_____

What are you wanting to do, after exploring the varied options presented in this book, to help you make the choice that is the best for your mental health?

_____

_____

_____

Is this choice based on your own decisions and not on someone else's (e.g., your NPD abuser)?

_____

How will you know you have successfully accomplished your choice?

_____

_____

_____

A key factor to this theory is that you are not to lose heart if you devise a plan to work toward obtaining your desires and it is not successful. You can always create a new plan of action and try again. It is not a one-and-done situation. It can take some time to effectively adapt your behaviors to those that help you successfully achieve your wants. Remember that the choice is yours and no one else's. This theory provides a wonderful segue into exploring your WDEP aspects regarding the type of relationship you now want with your NPD abuser.

Level of Contact

I know you are likely thinking about what I chose to do with my NPD abusive relationship. At first, I was even reluctant to share what choice I'd made, as I did not want to influence any reader's decision on this, but I believe in authenticity and so decided to share my decision about how I proceeded in my relationship. But first, I think it would be helpful to provide some context regarding the events surrounding my decision, especially since we just explored choice theory.

For years, I've harbored an on-off internal battle regarding the choices for how to proceed with my NPD abuser. At first, I did not conceptualize my treatment as abuse but, rather, felt it was something I needed to cope with—that it was my job to not cause any conflict. I stayed in the relationship and sought to keep the peace for many years. Unfortunately, due to the nature of NPD, peace was not very common. There were always tumultuous situations where I'd be put in the role of villain or troublemaker or told I'd caused harm. After being told that over and over, I decided to slowly disconnect from my NPD abuser and maintain a superficial relationship. It was very challenging, as I would have to work up the energy to connect for a holiday, birthday, or even a monthly call. Each time, I would get an overwhelming feeling of anxiety. I lived my life constantly on edge, unsure what might unfold next. Meanwhile, I shared the feelings I was experiencing with my husband because I had no friends who could fully understand the emotional turmoil I was in. At this point in my life, I was maintaining my relationship with my NPD abuser at a superficial level. I learned from years of experience that being superficial could protect me, for if I shared too much personal information, it would be used against me or be twisted in some way. I wanted to protect my family and me. Even with the superficial contact (commonly referred to as low contact), I constantly felt apprehensive. I was cautious about sharing events, school projects, work news, travel plans, and celebrations. I had learned from experience that my NPD abuser would stalk and watch us, then skew whatever information she'd learned to slander me and my family, thus manipulating others into perceiving us as bad or even evil.

The low contact was effective for several years, but family members frequently attempted to guilt me about my choice to keep a distance. It was very challenging to explain my choice in guarding my life from my NPD abuser because the abuser was very good at manipulating the outside public into believing I was the problem; absurdly, I was referred to as the "prodigal child" when, in fact, I was just maintaining healthy boundaries. There were so many negative comments, false stories, and attempts to ruin my reputation that I had no way to defend all the accusations. It was heart-wrenching at times, but the love of my husband and children, as well as the varied tools I've explored in this book, kept me grounded. I know many of you can relate to other's inability to fully comprehend that a mother, my NPD abuser, could wreak such havoc in their child's life. The outside world viewed my low contact as disrespectful, unloving, and selfish, but the bystander's view knew none of the abuse I had endured. This, along with my own sense of duty and guilt, kept me in low contact.

So what changed my mind and made me decide to take the next step? It was the perpetuation of multiple lies shared to new family members coupled with the absence of any desire to have an honest conversation with me about ways to resolve our relationship. I attempted to have a conversation with my NPD abuser after a year of navigating my own healing path of reflection. This conversation unfolded after I'd thoroughly discussed it with my husband and after much journaling and meditating. I was cautiously optimistic about the outcome. Well, I was glad I was finally having the conversation. In my attempt to have a conversation that was honest, transparent, and healing, the wrath unfolded. Within less than a minute of starting our conversation, I was immediately blamed for all the problems in our relationship, told I was a horrible and shameful person, and degraded in many ways. After listening to the berating while trying to inquire about a way to mend our relationship, I decided to let her know that I would no longer be speaking to her for my own mental health. As I write this sentence, it has been 8 years since I made that statement. I am sure some reading this let out a gasp on seeing that number, but for others, it may have been a sigh of relief, as it's provided you with support for your decision to go no contact.

I'm sure you've noticed the use of the terms *low contact* and *no contact*. There is also the choice of *full contact*. It is important to break down all three so you can make an effective choice as you implement the elements I explored with you regarding WDEP (Glasser 1999; 2013). I would like for you to consider the thoughts that emerge when you read these.

Full contact: 100% involvement at superficial and deep levels of interaction

Low contact: partial involvement but primarily at a superficial level of interaction

No contact: no involvement at either a superficial or deeper level of interaction

After your reflection/first thoughts, I ask you to consider what each of these might represent in your life. When we are in full contact with someone in our life, there is consistent engagement across varied domains of life. There is not only superficial conversation but very deep conversation. Examples of superficial conversation include talking about the day, the weather, daily events, and so forth. With a deeper conversation, there is the potential to talk about work, family, health, frustrations, dreams, and concerns. I often consider full contact as a way to explore all of life's elements with someone— without secrets—and it involves actively listening to each other. Moreover, this suggests you are heard by your receiver without judgment and without the shared information being used against you.

It is easy to see how staying in full contact with an NPD abuser might lead to disaster over time, as they need to be the center of attention, and the information you share can be used as a weapon against you. If your relationship stays in full-contact mode, you will endure continual upheaval, which will likely leave you feeling dismissed, gaslit, misunderstood, and overcome by various emotions, including fear. Having spent most of my life in full contact, I always felt I had to watch my back for the next bad thing that would happen. I would battle feeling guilty for not wanting to connect to my NPD abuser, but then after connecting, I'd feel depleted, was filled with self-loathing, and harbored the desire to avoid. This unhealthy pattern was evident in my life for many years. There is no way I can truly convey all the experiences I'd had while in full contact or the overwhelming negative impact it had on my whole life. I am sure you can relate to that, and I ask you to reflect on your own experience of full contact. Consider not only the experiences but also the toll on your thoughts, emotions, behaviors, and physiology. I know for me, it shaped everything about my life.

It took some time for me to move toward a plan to go low contact. This type of interaction can look different and will depend upon the relationship dynamics. The low contact that I developed with my NPD abuser provided a lot of relief. At first, the low contact would be instigated by a disagreement where my NPD abuser told me I was in the wrong and then would not talk to me again until I'd apologized. This resulted in spans of time without contact that ranged anywhere from a month up to a year. I would always end up feeling guilty and apologizing, even when I knew I had done nothing wrong. But I felt pressure to be the one to approach the relationship, as it was my family and I didn't want to lose them. Having a mother with NPD creates layers upon layers of emotional turmoil. When I had the distance, I felt a sense of relief, but then the guilt would build up over time. These breaks in the relationship made it easier to shift to superficial relationship that was less frequent. Having a shallow relationship saved me a lot of heartache. You can define superficial and shallow from your own perspective, but for me, it meant keeping the conversation to daily living skills and not going deeper into any thoughts, emotions, or concerns that were in my life. It was truly inauthentic, but it was a means of self-protection and boundary setting, and it allowed me to have peace of mind and distance between interactions. Consider if it is possible for you to go low contact. If so, do you want to go low contact? What would low contact look like for you?

The moment I decided to have what I referred to as my final conversation, I knew I would have to put distance between my NPD abuser and me. There was no way I could continue in a relationship where I desired authenticity but was only receiving a blasting of my character and my flaws without any reciprocated self-reflection or acknowledgment of her own imperfections. I have to reiterate that going no contact was the hardest decision I have ever made, and it caused me intense emotional pain. In fact, when I made the decision to go no contact, I was not sure how long I could go without talking to my mom. But as I engaged in more self-reflection, reflected on my life, examined the relationship from varied angles, read, researched, and went through counseling, I knew I needed to maintain no contact.

When I went no contact with my NPD mom, this also meant I had to sever relationship with my father. It shifted the relationship with my siblings and left me as an orphan. As I began to investigate others who'd gone no contact, I came across the idea of purposeful orphaning. I liked this term, as it alludes to the power of choice. I chose to disconnect for my own mental well-being versus having been orphaned by my parents. I experience emotional pain and sometimes wishful thinking that things could be different, but I know it will never be. This mode of no contact can be misleading, as the outside world thinks this means I do not love my parents and do not forgive them. This is not true. We can have love at a distance, and as you remember from a previous chapter, forgiveness is frequently given from a distance. It is rare to receive an apology or an acknowledgment of harmful behavior from an abuser, so forgiveness usually has to be offered without having received an apology first. Narcissists do not apologize anyway (unless to manipulate).

It is a huge decision to go no contact, so we need to discern if it is right for us. Not everyone who is in an NPD relationship makes the decision to go no contact. There are some individuals who choose to go low contact, others who have limited choices, and still others who do not desire to disconnect and wish to stay in full contact. This is one of the hardest decisions you will make, so exploring the WDEP (Glasser, 1999; 2013) aspects are important to making this choice. It is difficult not only because of the change in the relationship but also because there are "flying monkeys" who will try to sway you. In the world of narcissism, the term flying monkeys refers to the monkeys in the movie *The Wizard of Oz*; they are sent by the witch to spy on Dorothy. Narcissists will send their flying monkeys to inundate your life and see what is going on in your world. They may message you on social media, text your phone, call you, or even swing by for a visit. It will come unexpectedly. Take this sudden connection as a signal that the narcissist is trying to find a way to investigate your life. Other things might occur in the background (e.g., a rumor is spread about you), or there is a heightened attempt to reach out at first, and you may need to block the numbers of the unhealthy people in your life. However, going no contact can become very peaceful over time. It is normal to take appreciable time to think further about your decision. Guilt is one of the major reasons individuals won't choose low contact or no contact.

We have explored guilt before, but I bring this up again because the feeling of guilt drives so many of our behaviors. I know that for years, I felt a heightened sense of guilt anytime I thought about going low contact, causing me to vacillate with the decision. Once I finally went low contact, I continued to be subjected to various forms of emotional abuse, manipulation, lies, and deceit, which I also took with moments of laughs and smiles, but then the cycle would revert back to harmful behavior. This is reminiscent of the cycle of violence I explored with you in Chapter 10. When I went no contact, I underwent a variety of emotions, including intense sadness, grief, worry, and guilt. I had to remind myself—and I still do at times—that I have not done anything wrong by making this choice and that it was not a decision I made lightly. When guilt emerges, I typically do a meditation, journal, practice mindfulness to access my intuition, talk to my spouse, and get myself grounded. I've learned to ask myself, Is this true guilt or false guilt?

True guilt is the guilt that results from breaking your personal values or morals, or deontological guilt. An example might be someone who's been raised to not bully, and yet they make fun of someone less fortunate or who is different. If they then feel an overwhelming sense of guilt later, it is likely because this person broke their own personal values around how to treat others. Altruistic guilt is the empathic guilt that comes from causing harm to someone else, which includes stealing, lying, or even causing physical harm (intentionally or not). This guilt that emerges is due to someone actually causing another person harm. Thinking on these two types of guilt, you may quickly recognize that your NPD abuser has not expressed any guilt—and you would be accurate. I hope you're also processing that your decision to go low or no contact should not evoke either kind of guilt—that is, unless you value staying in abusive relationships, which you likely do not. You probably have been brainwashed to believe that this type of abuse is normal.

False guilt, sometimes referred to as undeserved guilt, is a sense of guilt that has typically been ignited by your NPD abuser, as well as others in your life who have an ulterior motive for evoking guilt in you. This typically arises when people feel guilty for doing something that isn't actually wrong or bad. It may be perceived as wrong or bad in the eyes of the individual receiving the word "no" or an enforced boundary. These realities of saying no and setting boundaries are not morally wrong, and they do not cause harm. Sometimes, we can develop false guilt due to the unfolding of events that are out of our control. For example, you set a boundary with your NPD abuser and then go low contact. Three weeks after you go low contact, you find out that person got in a car accident and had broken a few bones. There is no correlation between you going low contact, setting your boundary, and this accident happening, but you may very well feel it is connected. When this false guilt emerges, you need to go back over the strategies outlined in this book and practice them to adjust your self-talk, regulate your emotions, and help yourself be free of this unnecessary guilt.

Hopefully, this chapter has helped you see that you are never too far down a road to make a change. We always have a choice, but we need to examine what factors contribute to our choices in life. Ensuring our basic needs are met and honestly evaluating what we are searching for in our relationships will help us make decisions that are right for us based on our own experiences. These choices should not be based on false or undeserved guilt but on a careful evaluation of what is most effective, whether that is full contact, low contact, or no contact. Another way to discern your level of contact is through detachment. According to Melody Beattie, "detachment is releasing, or detaching from, a person or problem in love" (Beattie, 1992, p. 62). Let that sink in as this chapter ends. Ask yourself, What level of connection do I want? The power is in your hands.

$\backsim$

References

Chapter 2

Ainsworth, M. D., & Bell, S. M. (1970). Attachment, exploration and separation: Illustrated by the behavior of one-year olds in a strange situation. *Child Development, 41*(1), 49–67. https://doi.org/10.2307/1127388

American Counseling Association. (2014). ACA code of ethics. American Counseling Association.

American Psychiatric Association. (2022). *Diagnostic and statistical manual of mental disorders: DSM-5TR.* (5th ed.). American Psychiatric Association.

Barnert, E. S., Perry, R., Shetgiri, R., Steers, N., Dudovitz, R., Heard-Garris, N., Zima, B., & Chung, P. (2021). Adolescent protective and risk factors for incarceration through early adulthood. *J Child Fam Stud 30,* 1428–1440. https://doi.org /10.1007/s10826-021-01954-y

Bowlby, J. (1969). *Attachment and loss.* Basic Books.

Butcher, J. N., Dahstrom, W. G., Graham, J. R., Tellegen, A., & Kaemmer, B. (1989). *The Minnesota Multiphasic Personality Inventory-2 (MMPI-2): Manual for administration and scoring.* University of Minnesota Press.

Hoertel, N., Peyre H., Lavaud P., Blanco, C., Guerin-Langlois, C., René, M., Schuster, J. P., Lemogne, C., Delorme, R., & Limosin F. (2018). Examining sex differences in DSM-IV-TR narcissistic personality disorder symptom expression using Item Response Theory (IRT). *Psychiatry Research, 160,* 500–507. https://doi .org/10.1016/j.psychres.2017.12.031

Lawrence, K. C., & Nkoane, M. M. (2020). Transforming higher education spaces: Analysis of higher educational attainment expectation factors among high school learners in Kwa-Dlangezwa, South Africa. *International Journal of Education and Practice, 8*(3), 547– 556. https://doi.org/10.18488/journal.61.2020.83.547.556

Raskin, R. & Hall, C. S. (1979). A narcissistic personality inventory. *Psychological Reports, 45*,590.

Stanton, K., & Zimmerman, M. (2018). Clinician ratings of vulnerable and grandiose narcissistic features: Implications for an expanded narcissistic personality disorder diagnosis. *Personality Disorders: Theory, Research, and Treatment, 9*(3), 263–272. https://doi.org/10.1037/per0000272

Chapter 3

Ainsworth, M. D. (1964). Patterns of attachment behavior shown by the infant in interaction with his mother. *Merrill-Palmer Quarterly of Behavior and Development, 10*, 51–58.

Ainsworth, M. D. S., Blehar, M. C., Waters, E., & Wall, S. (1978). *Patterns of attachment: A psychological study of the strange situation.* Erlbaum.

American Psychological Association. (2018). Deprivation. In APA *dictionary of psychology.* https://dictionary.apa.org/deprivation

American Psychiatric Association. (2022). *Diagnostic and statistical manual of mental disorders: DSM-5TR.* (5th ed.). American Psychiatric Association.

American Psychological Association. (2023). Caregiving. In APA *dictionary of psychology.* https://dictionary.apa.org/caregiver

Beattie, M. (1992). *Codependent no more: How to stop controlling others and start caring for yourself* (2nd ed.). Hazelden.

Bowlby, J. (1969). *Attachment and loss: Vol. 1. Loss.* Basic Books.

Bowlby, J. (1958). The nature of the child's tie to his mother. *International Journal of Psychoanalysis, XXXIX,* 1–23. Bowlby J. (1988). *A secure base: Parent-child attachment and healthy human development.* Tavistock/Routledge.

Bowlby, J., Aimsowrth, M., Bosont, M., & Rosenbluth, D. (1956). The effects of mother-child separation: A follow up study. *British Journal Medical Psychology, 29,* 211–247.

Centers for Disease Control and Prevention. (2020). *Fast facts: Preventing adverse childhood experiences.* U.S. Department of Health and Human Services. https://www.cdc.gov/violenceprevention/aces/fastfact.html

Harlow, H. F. (1958). The nature of love. *American Psychologist, 13*(12), 673–685. https://doi.org/10.1037/h0047884

Rahim, M., & Katz, J. (2019). Forty years of conflict: The effects of gender and generational on conflict-management strategies. *International Journal of Conflict Management, 31*(1), 1–16.

Savery, D. C. (2018). *Echoism: The silenced response to narcissism.* Routledge.

Chapter 4

Beckett, C., & Taylor, H. (2019). *Human growth and development* (4th ed.). Sage.

Darabont, F. (Director). (1994). *Shawshank Redemption* [Film]. Warner Brothers.

Prochaska, J. O., & DiClemente, C. C. (1983). Stages and processes of self-change of smoking: Toward an integrative model of change. *Journal of Consulting and Clinical Psychology, 51*(3), 390–395. http://dx.doi.org/10.1037/0022-006X.51.3.390

Chapter 5

Bruner, J. S. (2002). *Making stories: Law, literature, life.* Farrar, Straus and Giroux.

Landrum, R. E., Brakke, K., & McCarthy, M. A. (2019). The pedagogical power of storytelling. *Scholarship of Teaching and Learning in Psychology, 5*(3), 247–253. https://doi.org/10.1037/stl0000152

Prochaska, J. O., & DiClemente, C. C. (1983). Stages and processes of self-change of smoking: Toward an integrative model of change. *Journal of Consulting and Clinical Psychology, 51*(3), 390–395. http://dx.doi.org/10.1037/0022-006X.51.3.390

Watson, J. B. (1924). *Psychology: From the standpoint of a behaviorist* (2nd ed.). J. B. Lippincott.

Chapter 6

Hayes, S. C., Strosahl, K. D., & Wilson, K. G. (2016). *Acceptance and commitment therapy: The process and practice of mindful change* (2nd ed.). Guilford Press.

Perls, F. (1992). *Gestalt therapy verbatim.* The Gestalt Journal Press.

Smith, M. J. (1975). *When I say no, I feel guilty: How to cope using the skills of systematic assertive therapy.* Bantam Books.

Vella, S. -L. C. & Pai, N. B. (2019). A theoretical review of psychological resilience: Defining resilience and resilience research over the decades. *Archives of Medicine and Health Sciences 7*(2), 233–239. https://doi.org/10.4103/amhs.amhs_119_19

White, M. (2007). *Maps of narrative practice.* W. W. Norton.

Chapter 7

Dahl, C., & Davidson, R. (2019). Mindfulness and the contemplative life: pathways to connection, insight, and purpose. *ScienceDirect, 28,* 60–64. https://doi.org/10.1016/j.copsyc.2018.11.007

Demnitz-King, H., Gonneaud, J., Klimecki, O. M., Chocat, A., Collette, F., Dautricourt, S., Jessen, F., Krolak-Salmon, P., Lutz, A., Morse, R., Molinuevo, J., Poisnel, G., Touron, E., Wirth, M., Walker, Z., Chételat, G., Marchant, N., & Medit-Ageing Research Group. (2022). Association of self-reflection with cognition and brain health in cognitively unimpaired older adults. *Neurology, 99*(13), e1422–e1431. https://doi.org/10.1212/WNL.0000000000200951

Kabat-Zinn, J. (1994). *Wherever you go there you are: Mindfulness meditation in everyday life.* Hyperion.

Linehan, M. (2015). *DBT skills training manual.* (2nd ed.). The Guilford Press.

Shapero, B. G., Greenberg, J., Pedrelli, P., De Jong, M., & Desbordes, G. (2018). Mindfulness-based interventions in psychiatry. *Focus: American Psychiatric Publishing, 16* (1), 32–39.

Chapter 8

Cuddy, A. (2012, June). *Your body language may shape who you are* [Video]. TED Conferences. https://www.ted.com/talks/amy_cuddy_your_body_language_may_shape_who_you_are

Greenberg, L. S. (2017). Introduction. In L. S. Greenberg (Ed.), *Emotion-focused therapy* (Revised ed., pp. 3–11). American Psychological Association. https://doi.org/10.1037/15971-001

Linehan, M. (2015). *DBT skills training handouts and worksheets* (2nd ed.). Guilford Press.

Petric, D. (2022) The introvert-ambivert-extrovert spectrum. *Open Journal of Medical Psychology, 11*(3), 103–111. https://doi.org/10.4236/ojmp.2022.113008

Chapter 9

Beck, A. (1976). *Cognitive therapy and the emotional disorders: A major exploration of an influential approach to the understanding and treatment of mental illness.* International University Press.

Ellis, A. (2023). *Overcoming destructive beliefs, feelings, and behaviors: New directions for rational emotive behavior therapy* (2nd ed.). Prometheus. (Original work published 2001)

Linehan, M. (2015). *DBT Skills Training Handouts and Worksheets.* (2nd ed.). The Guilford Press.

Chapter 10

Beck, A. T. (2005). The current state of cognitive therapy: A 40-year retrospective. *Archives of General Psychiatry, 62*(9), 953–959. https://doi.org/10.1001/archpsyc.62.9.953

Casagrande, M., Forte, G., Favieri, F., Agostini, F., Giovannoli, J., Arcari, L., Passaseo, I., Semeraro, R., Camastra, G., Langher, V., Pazzaglia, M., & Cacciotti, L. (2021). The broken heart: The role of life events in takotsubo syndrome. *Journal of Clinical Medicine, 10*(21), 4940. https://doi.org/10.3390/jcm10214940

Forte, G., Favieri, F., & Casagrande, M. (2019). Heart rate variability and cognitive function: A systematic review. *Front Neuroscience*, *13*, 710. https://doi.org/10.1001/10.3389/fnins.2019.00710

Hooda, V. S., Muly, P. A., Muley, P. P., Anjankar, A., & Bandre, G. (2024). Effect of exercise on depression, anxiety and mood: A narrative review. *Journal of Clinical and Diagnostic Research*, *18*(1), 1–04. https://doi.org/10.7860/JCDR/2024/65557.18929

Linehan, M. (2015). *DBT skills training handouts and worksheets*. (2nd ed.). The Guilford Press.

Pence, E., & Paymar, M. (1993). *Education groups for men who batter: The Duluth model*. Springer Publishing.

Thayer, J. F., Åhs, F., Fredrikson, M., Sollers, J. J., III, & Wager, T. D. (2012). A meta-analysis of heart rate variability and neuroimaging studies: Implications for heart rate variability as a marker of stress and health. *Neuroscience Biobehavior*, *36*(2), 747–756. https://doi.org/10.1016/j.neubiorev.2011.11.009

Torres, V. (2023). Multigenerational clinical history of a family with several members carrying narcissistic personality disorder. *International Journal of Social Science and Human Research*, *6*(5), 2644–0695. https://doi.org/10.47191/ijsshr/v6-i5-28

Walker, L. (1979). *The battered woman*. Harper & Row.

Chapter 11

Akhtar, S., & Barlow, J. (2018). Forgiveness therapy for the promotion of mental well-being: A systematic review and meta-analysis. *Trauma, Violence, & Abuse*, *19*(1), 107–122. https://doi.org/10.1177/1524838016637079

Anderson, J. C., Linden, W., & Habra, M. E. (2006). Influence of apologies and trait hostility on recovery from anger. *Journal of Behavioral Medicine*, *29*, 347–358.

Chandler, C. K., Holden, J. J., & Kolander, C. A. (1992). Counseling spiritual wellness: Theory and practice. *Journal of Counseling & Development*, *71*, 168–175. https://doi.org/10.1002/j.1556-6676.1992.tb02193.x

Enright, R. D. (2001). *Forgiveness is a choice*. APA Books.

Enright, R. D. (2012). *The forgiving life: A pathway to overcoming resentment and creating a legacy of love*. APA Books.

Enright, R. D., & Coyle, C. T. (1998). Researching the process model of forgiveness within psychological interventions. In E. L. Worthington Jr. (Ed), *Dimensions of forgiveness: Psychological research and theological perspective* (pp. 139–162). Temple Foundation Press.

Enright, R. D., Freedman, S., & Rique, J. (1998). The psychology of interpersonal forgiveness. In R. D. Enright & J. North (Eds.), *Exploring forgiveness* (pp. 46–62). University of Wisconsin Press.

Enright, R. D., Santos, M. J., & Al-Mabuk, R. (1989). The adolescent as forgiver. *Journal of Adolescence*, *12*(1), 95–110. https://doi.org/10.1016/0140-1971(89)90092-4

Fincham, F. D. (2022). Towards a psychology of divine forgiveness. *Psychology of Religion and Spirituality, 14*(4), 451–461. https://doi.org/10.1037/rel0000323

Jones, J. (2023, September 22). In U.S., 47% identify as religious, 33% as spiritual. *Gallup*. https://news.gallup.com/poll/511133/identify-religious-spiritual.aspx#

Kauppi, K., Vanhala, A., Roos, E., & Torkki, P. (2023). Assessing the structures and domains of wellness models: A systematic review. *International Journal of Wellbeing, 13*(2), 1–19. https://doi.org/10.5502/ijw.v13i2.2619

Myers, J., Sweeney, T., & Witmer, M. (2000). The wheel of wellness counseling for wellness: A holistic model for treatment planning. *Journal of Counseling and Development, 78*(3), 251–266.

Oxford English Dictionary. (2023). Forgiveness (n.). In *Oxford English Dictionary*. https://doi.org/10.1093/OED/6847027460

Seward, B. L. (1995). Reflections on human spirituality for the worksite. *American Journal of Health Promotion, 9*(3), 165–168. https://doi.org/10.4278/0890-1171-9.3.165

Van Tongeren, D., Green, J., Hook, J., Davis, D., Davis, J., & Ramos, M. (2015). Forgiveness increases the meaning of life. *Social Psychological and Personality Science, 6*(1), 47–55. https://doi.org/10.1177/1948550614541298

Walrond-Skinner, S. (1998). The function and role of forgiveness in working with couples and families: Clearing the ground. *Journal of Family Therapy, 20*(1), 3–19. https://doi.org/10.1111/1467-6427.00065

Worthington, E. L. (2005). *Handbook of Forgiveness*. Brunner-Routledge.

Chapter 12

Beattie, M. (1992). *Codependent no more: How to stop controlling others and start caring for yourself* (2nd ed.). Hazelden.

Glasser, W. (1999). *Choice theory. A new psychology of personal freedom*. Harper Collins.

Glasser, W. (2013). *Take charge of your life: How to get what you need with choice theory psychology* (2nd ed.). iUniverse.

Moreno, J. L. (1934). *Who shall survive? A new approach to the problems of human interrelations*. Nervous and Mental Disease Publishing.

Index

~

About the Author

Rosanne Nunnery, PhD, LPC-S, NCC, BC-TMH, C-DBT, CGP, earned a PhD in counselor education with an emphasis in community counseling and a minor in educational leadership. She holds a master's degree in community counseling and is a licensed professional counselor and supervisor in Mississippi. Her extensive qualifications include being a national certified counselor, a board-qualified supervisor in Mississippi, a board-certified telemental health counselor, a certified DBT treatment team leader, and a certified grief professional.

Since 2000, Dr. Nunnery has been a practicing counselor, expanding her role to counselor-educator in 2011 and telemental health counselor in 2017. As an associate clinical professor, she is involved in teaching graduate courses, serving on various committees, publishing supervising students, consulting, and counseling under Nunnery Clinical and Educational Consulting, LLC.

Her professional services extend to working with diverse adult clientele and contributing to multiple association committees. Notably, she has served on the American Counseling Association (ACA) Ethics Committee, volunteered for the Mississippi Counselors Association for Spiritual, Ethical Values in Counseling (MASERVIC) as president, and participated in the Association for Spiritual, Ethical, and Religious Values in Counseling (ASERVIC) Ethics and Values Committee. Additionally, she has chaired the ethics committee for the Mississippi Counseling Association (MCA) and was recently elected to faculty senate at Mississippi State University.

Dr. Nunnery has presented at the local, state, and national levels on topics related to spirituality, wellness, personality disorders, DBT, complicated grief, ethics, depression, anxiety, trauma, narcissistic abuse, and other theoretical applications. In 2023 she coedited and published a book entitled *Telemental Health: What Every Student Needs to Know*. She is currently under contract with a coeditor to produce a book on personality disorders from a systemic perspective—a passion project from her own experience and work with clients. She advocates on behalf of counselors in training self-efficacy, wellness, evidence-based practice, and ethical practice.

~

Extra Journal Pages